C000092480

SHAKESPEARE
The Four Romances

SHAKESPEARE

The Four Romances

ROBERT M. ADAMS

W · W · NORTON & COMPANY

New York   London

Copyright © 1989 by Robert M. Adams
All rights reserved.
Published simultaneously in Canada by Penguin Books Canada Ltd.,
2801 John Street,
Markham, Ontario L3R 1B4.
Printed in the United States of America.

The text of this book is composed in 10/13 Palatino, with
display type set in Palatino.
Composition by PennSet, Inc.

Book design by Jacques Chazaud.

First Edition

Library of Congress Cataloging-in-Publication Data
Adams, Robert Martin, 1915–
Shakespeare—the four romances.
Includes bibliographical references.
1. Shakespeare, William, 1564–1616—Tragicomedies.
I. Title.
PR2981.5.A33   1989   822.3'3   88-19561

ISBN: 978-0-393-33690-0

W. W. Norton & Company, Inc., 500 Fifth Avenue,
New York, N.Y. 10110
W. W. Norton & Company Ltd., 37 Great Russell Street,
London WC1B 3NU

1 2 3 4 5 6 7 8 9 0

CONTENTS

† †

PRINCIPLES:
A FOREWORD

Working over a field as thoroughly gleaned as Shakespeare, one can't hope to do more than summarize long-standing opinions and arrange them in a provisional, perhaps useful, pattern, while adding, with a little bit of luck, a detail here and a point of emphasis there. One of our most inventive and highly organized critics, when asked what was the use of his elegant, intricate system, answered briefly and sufficiently, "It's a mnemonic device." I claim no loftier function for my study of the Shakespearean romances, and don't doubt that anyone who succeeds in arranging these four plays and their rainbow of interpretive theories into a pattern the mind can grasp and the memory retain will have served most of his readers well.

Modern theory and the record of much modern critical practice emphasize alike the supreme value of the critic's original insights, achieved sometimes to the advantage, sometimes at the expense, of the text on which he comments. This could be called the power of positive insight into either text or self, and it has been exercised to expand many-fold our awareness of myriad-minded Shakespeare, his millefol-

iate imagination, his polyvalent language—and our awareness of our awareness. Spontaneous as mushrooms, possible
approaches to Shakespeare proliferate daily, to entangle the
interpreter in a labyrinth of methodological alternatives, long
before his text even heaves over the horizon. His pretence
to be an individual formulating his own views, on Shakespeare or anything else, can hardly hope to survive a first
plunge into "the literature." Yet it has been said there is an
art to wash clean in dirty water; if so, its time has surely
arrived in the late 20th century. As we learn to recognize the
world's muddy commonplaces even in the wellspring of our
own meditations, it is the rinsing of the inner eye that we
ought to attempt. The way down and in may take us almost
as far as the road up and out.

A clutter of overscribbled commentary is nothing new.
Analysis and interpretation of Shakespeare have a labyrinthine history which, like most labyrinths, combines a sense
of infinite variety with a sense of eternal recurrence. For a
long time the romances—being clearly different from the
sorts of plays Shakespeare had previously written—were cut
down and judged, as inferior work, to require some special
explanation, biographical or cultural. When the notion
caught on, starting with the romantics and gaining momen-
tum through the 19th and early 20th century, that the plays
might be allegorical or symbolic in their action, and therefore
deliberately fragile as represented stories in order to invite a
larger imaginative vision, wide expanses of interpretive liberty opened up. Personal and confessional intimations, moral
teachings in the prophetic mode, visionary exaltations, and
semi-mystical numinous wisdom swam within the interpreters' ken. Enriched meanings for the romances (sometimes avowedly Christian, more often incorporating elements
of myth and ritual from comparative anthropology alongside
concepts from depth psychology with a flavoring of linguistic
theory) deepened and certainly rendered more serious dis-

cussion of the plays. From the first, a strain of astringent historically-minded criticism tried to restrict the meanings to be discovered in Shakespeare's plays to concepts and constructs of which his contemporaries (meaning specifically his audiences) showed themselves aware. In recent years, i.e., the last quarter-century, the allegorical/symbolic mode of reading Shakespeare has been subject to acerbic criticism without much extra authority having accrued to the severely historical approach. The time therefore seems right to go at the texts with a minimum of methodological apparatus, if only to find out how far one can get that way. This study proposes itself not as a closed conclusion, but as an investigation.

The text, accordingly, holds aloof from polemic, and does not even list most of the many ingenious and intricate approaches that it has deliberately forborne. Like everyone else who writes on Shakespeare I owe an enormous debt to my predecessors, not least to those from whom I have chosen, in the end, to dissent; but as I have done a minimum of challenging, so I have held down on applause and approbation. A list of the major sources consulted, with a brief indication of their general character where appropriate, is appended to each chapter. But detailed footnoting—oppressive to most, unnecessary to many, and a convenience for only a few—has been curtailed.*

The plays are not paraphrased or summarized in this study. I write with the texts in front of me, and recommend that the reader, if he doesn't have the plays sharply in mind,

---

* For texts of the plays particularly studied I have used the Arden Shakespeare issued by Methuen: *Pericles*, ed. F. D. Hoeniger; *Cymbeline*, ed. J. M. Nosworthy; *The Winter's Tale*, ed. J. H. Pafford; and *The Tempest*, ed. Frank Kermode. For general reference to Shakespeare, I have used the London Shakespeare in six volumes, ed. John Munro (Simon & Schuster, 1958) and Charlton Hinman's *The Norton Facsimile: The First Folio of Shakespeare* (Norton, 1968).

keep a text handy to refer to. Summarizing the plot of a play, like paraphrasing the "meaning" of a poem, provides an open invitation to twist it into the shape the critic finds most convenient. That has not been my aim. So far as possible, introductory comments and references to the specific passage set the stage for analysis, so it won't be hard to know what part of the play is being discussed. But filling and bridgework have been held down. The book has taken form as topical remarks on the plays' important aspects, as I defined them, extended as far as they seemed useful. Transitional connectives have been treated as optional; and where I had nothing to say, it seemed important to stop writing.

That Shakespeare was a very capable literary artist I have assumed without demonstration, and suppose that my readers will know it without being repeatedly reminded. A special variety of criticism tries to provide for readers an emotional equivalent to what the critic thinks the reader ought to feel in the presence of the text; the way to do this has generally lain through accumulated superlatives, ecstatic "appreciations," and awed invocation of religious images. This path too I have left untaken. Still another procedure, less popular now than it used to be, is character-analysis, i.e., the discussion of Shakespeare's *personae* on the tacit assumption that they are living people with an independent existence off the page or stage. This needs no disavowal. On the face of it, psychological analysis of the literary creator is less absurd than putting his characters on the couch, but I have avoided it (1) because it distracts from the plays which are the prime concern, (2) because it requires more intimate facts in a richer context of development than can be had, and (3) because, having been repeatedly attempted, it has yielded few and unimpressive results. Finally, though I think I have profited peripherally from some of the theories loosely grouped as "deconstructionism," I have not been persuaded to adopt either them or any of their specialized vocabularies. Whatever the metaphysics of *écriture*, its pursuit cannot compensate for the blocking effect of placing the opaque and often ungainly critic in front of the translucent and delicate text. This study tries to let the plays speak through it.

A rule of thumb I learned from reading Yeats seems to apply equally to Shakespeare: the best gloss on one passage of the poet may well be another passage of the same poet. Though not very precise, this has appealed to me as a lead worth following, but it comes with an important corollary—that abuse of the process can easily slide into the malpractice to be known as synoptic reading. The synoptic reader surrounds passage A with parallel or related passages B, C, D, etc., then rings passage B with a necklace of A, C, D, and so forth. Thus, by reinforcing each single passage with as many of the others as he chooses, the commentator is able to impose on his text a wide range of emphases, all of his own choosing. This technique, rendered almost too easy by use of concordance and computer, has the special advantage that one seems to be adding no extraneous material, since everything one imports is warranted Shakespeare. But what the hidden controller manipulates is the importance of his chosen themes; and this too I have tried to avoid.

The approach of this study, for which I disclaim in advance all originality, has been to look on the plays as verbal contrivances designed to create effects on audiences. I presume neither to define any one audience as inherently better than the others, nor to propose one effect as correct at the expense of the rest. But some effects may, by comparison/contrast with others or with different contexts, be judged more probable or more rich in significant implications. From a variety of different sources we know a good deal about Shakespeare's audiences, something about the range of allusion to which they were open, a little bit about the values they brought to the playhouse. From the spectrum of Shakespearean plays we can learn something of the playwright's techniques, his patterns of imagery, the situations to which his work most often recurs. We have also, to guide or bewilder us, a long record of stage-performances, of critical commentary, and the climate, such as it is, of modern opinion. The present age is neither more nor less privileged than any other in its approach to truth; but in its approach to living experience it is, for the moment, privileged—which also means "constrained"; even in pretending to be other than we are, we cannot relinquish the thought-habits of our quotidian selves.

Amid all these generalizations, if the commentator on Shakespeare is menaced by one spook more vast and intangible than the others, it is the demon of the commonplace. "Oh," says Montaigne, "what a sweet and soft and healthy pillow is ignorance and incuriosity, to rest a well-made head!" But mere ignorance is for most an uncomfortably empty pillowcase, the true sleep-producing stuffing of which is *idées reçues*. Apart from writing unintelligibly, the safest guard against such insidious comforts is a canine mistrust of the self-guided pencil and the ready formula. But such mistrust is a private instinct; it has not yet been built into word-processors, even of the best Japanese manufacture.

It's quite possible that I've pitched my critical principles too high to be able to live up to them myself. That has happened before. But the comfortable book on Shakespeare is one of those not worth writing.

For the benefit of readers trapped in the contemporary habit of using the word "romance" to mean a dreamy, erotic tale, let it be prefixed that here the word has a less specific but very different meaning. It is approximately a story of search or quest in which a wanderer, displaced for one reason or other, seeks a goal which, if only for purposes of the tale, is accepted as ultimate. This is only the vaguest and most indefinite of gestures toward an immense and complicated region of narrative by which Shakespeare's last four plays were touched. The first chapter takes a few further steps toward a historical definition of romances as they were known to Shakespeare; for a brief, brilliant, panoramic survey of the different origins, varieties, and tonalities of romance, the reader is referred to the article on "Romance" by George Saintsbury for the *Encyclopaedia Britannica*.

Robert M. Adams

SHAKESPEARE
The Four Romances

†††

I

BOUNDARIES

THE LAST FOUR PLAYS OF WILLIAM SHAKESPEARE FORM A
distinct group, similar to one another in several respects,
different from the other plays in several respects. They are
not, to be sure, absolutely the last work that Shakespeare
ever performed for the stage; pretty certainly, he did some
later collaborative writing with John Fletcher (and conceivably a third party) on *Henry VIII, The Two Noble Kinsmen*, and
perhaps a play, now lost, titled *Cardenio.** But at most his
participation in the three post-romance plays was limited to
particular scenes. Though *Henry VIII* was included in the
First Folio as entirely Shakespeare's, most later commentary
distinguishes two hands in it; assuming for the moment that
this is so, and taking for granted the major role of Fletcher
in *The Two Noble Kinsmen*, the four plays commonly desig-
nated "romances" are the last dramatic works for which
Shakespeare was responsible as a whole. Their titles are *Pericles, Cymbeline, The Winter's Tale*, and *The Tempest*. (Using the

---

* Discussion of these three plays, and Shakespeare's possible part in them,
is reserved for the appendix.

abbreviations proposed by Professor Hinman and now standard, they will be curtailed here to *Per.*, *Cym.*, *WT*, and *Tmp.*)
One of the four comes with a shabbier pedigree than the other three. *Per.* was not admitted to the First Folio and survives only in a set of very corrupt Quartos. The quality of the last three acts being different from that of the first two, double authorship has been suspected; but other explanations, such as different reporters, are possible. There is much that is problematic about this play; but the Quarto published in 1609 claimed the whole thing for Shakespeare, and that, given the brief lapse of time, justifies a conjecture that it must have been acted under his name. Its likeness in theme and structure to the other romances will be apparent to anyone who surveys the group of four. If admitted at all, it is the first of the set; approximate dates would be 1607 for *Per.*, 1609 for *Cym.*, 1610 for *WT*, and 1611 for *Tmp.* These are conjectural dates, arrived at by retreating a decent interval from the date of registry or first performance, as known by documentary evidence; they make no allowance for the possibility that these plays, like any other of Shakespeare's, may have been germinating in his mind or lying dormant in his notebooks for years before they took final shape. But, for what they are worth, the datings serve to group the romances together, and to separate them quite clearly from Shakespeare's previous plays: the last four before *Pericles* were, probably, *Coriolanus* (1607), *Timon of Athens* (1605?–08), *Antony and Cleopatra* (1606–07), and *King Lear* (1605).

To explain and confirm the classification, some of the common features of the romances may be briefly listed. In all four of the plays a major feature of the action is a royal child lost in infancy, deprived of rightful status, and after trials and dangers restored. Three of these lost children (heroines of *Per.*, *WT*, and *Tmp.*) are girls with strikingly similar names: Marina, Perdita, Miranda. Through the recovery of these girls (and the analogous reuniting of Imogen with her husband, while her two lost brothers are also recovered) the kingdom of their parents is restored to prosperity, unity, or spiritual health. Three of the plays (*Tmp.* excepted) are strikingly episodic in their construction; major events occur as a result of coincidence or accident, while characters of clear importance to the action disappear throughout several acts. In two of the plays a long period of time—more than a decade—passes in the interval between acts. Three of the four plays wander across extensive tracts of geographical distance—*Tmp.* is the exception again, but only partially so, for it is set in an exotic location to begin with. Characterization is not strongly marked, and the moral qualities of major persons have been described as schematic, which may be just another word for simplistic. Supernatural incidents often occur, rudimentary disguises must be accepted as impenetrable, and dramatic contrivance is often suspected. Interpolated music, actual masques, allegorical personages, and magic performances flesh out the romances. Most of the plays end with a scene of reconciliation and inclusion, from which not even the play's trouble-makers are excluded. Hardly any of these characteristics is absolutely peculiar to the romances, but collectively they give the four plays a very distinctive flavor.

Since they are effectually the last plays of Shakespeare, it's been natural for critics to ask in what relation the romances stand to the long line of plays that precede them, to define their special qualities in relation to their predecessors, and to ask why Shakespeare embarked on such a new path toward the end of his career. These questions partly overlap, and they lead directly into some very sticky speculations; one would prefer to bypass them. But the answers do much to define our subject, and the first step toward that subject is to lay out some textbook facts.

Shakespeare when he first started turning his mind toward romances about 1607 was 43 years old. He had been writing plays since the late 1580's, at a rate not far short of two plays per year. He had in addition been active as an actor and manager of his company, the most successful in London and consequently in the kingdom. For the greater part of his career in the theater he had occupied London lodgings, while his family remained in Stratford. The family consisted of his wife Anne (eight years his senior), a daughter Susanna (born 1583) and twins Judith and Hamnet (born 1585; Hamnet died in 1596). Apart from the two witty, Ovidian poems of 1593 and 1594 (*Venus and Adonis*, *The Rape of Lucrece*) and of course the long record of his successful plays, Shakespeare left a major document of the London years in the collection of 154 sonnets, first mentioned in 1598 and published without the author's consent in 1609. Some of these poems are clearly exercises on conventional Petrarchan or anti-Petrarchan themes, others clearly expressions of deep personal feelings. It is equally absurd to treat them as an autobiographical narrative and as a set of formal exercises. That they describe allusively a love affair containing a distinct homosexual component,* that they evoke two other shadowy erotic figures, a dark lady and a rival poet, hardly anybody can doubt. The full story is hard to make out, primarily because it isn't really a story; but in these tangled relationships, it seems clear, the poems plumb depths of remorse, agonies of jealousy, and the bitter resentments roused by ingratitude. Further than this, it's unnecessary to go. What happens in the sonnets (happens emotionally, of course; what happened in "real life" we shall never know) has little to do with the career of the playwright-businessman, nothing at all to do with the

---

* The second (1640) edition of the sonnets tried to heterosexualise some of them by altering key pronouns. More recently softening phrases like "an ideal young man" and "the renaissance cult of friendship" have been used to screen off an unacceptable reality. We are now in the stage of getting Shakespeare out of the closet—where, for sensible readers, he never was. A frank but unexaggerated picture is in gradual process of formation.

Stratford *paterfamilias*. The sonnets are mentioned here only in evidence that when the poet, some time around 1607 or 1608 began thinking about moving permanently to Stratford, more was involved than a simple change of address. In London he was leaving a society of high tensions, sharp contrasts, and cosmopolitan sophistication (such as England afforded)—of rich living, suave manners, peacock display, sexual adventure and misadventure, and perhaps cold duplicity as well. In Stratford he was returning to a countryside of bucolic peace and simplicity, where few of his neighbors read books and even fewer had ever visited a theater. He returned also to a 51-year-old wife, with whom his relations over the previous twenty years, though they may have been amicable, can scarcely have been intimate.

There is no implication in any of this toilsome circumstance that after London Stratford looked to Shakespeare like a prison, or that like Prospero returning to Milan, he expected every third thought to be of his grave. He was in his early forties; though nothing is known of his father's birthdate, John Shakespeare must have been at least in his seventies when he died in 1601. When he retired to Stratford, Shakespeare could naturally have anticipated much more than the period (less than a decade) that he was actually granted. Moreover, he had always had in mind to return to Stratford. Though he bought a bit of London real estate in 1613, that seems to have been an investment, not a residence; in Stratford, on the other hand, he bought several pieces of property, including, in 1597, the handsome house called New Place where his family, and later he himself, resided. Even before retiring, tradition eked out by supporting circumstance says he visited Stratford once a year. Yet the fact remains that retirement in one's early forties was as unusual then as it is today. After thirty-odd plays, he might well have felt drained; on the other hand, his contemporary Thomas Heywood, over a much longer career, claimed to have had a hand in over 200 dramas. Naturally, patching up a piece of claptrap like *The Four Prentices of London* is not exactly equivalent to writing *Hamlet* or *Lear*. But nothing suggests that the Shakespeare who had just produced *Antony*, and who still had before him four original plays as well as three collaborative ones, was entering into the shadows of senile impotence. So we are still left with the question, Was the removal to Stratford of a piece with the more or less contemporaneous shift to romance-writing? How intimate were the ties binding together these events? Indeed, passages can be found in the romances that seem to emphasize the greater authenticity of simple rural existence as contrasted with the polished insecurities of court life. In *Cym.* and *WT* the natural rectitude of provincials seems to be contrasted with the cynical duplicity of Italianate (i.e., cosmopolitan) sophistication. Autobiographical feelings might be concealed behind these passages, but then again they might not; the topics are frequent, not only in Shakespeare's earlier work but far and wide in Renaissance writing. Feelings of jealousy and resentment of ingratitude recur too often on the Shakespearean stage to provide evidence of any particular biographical crisis in or near 1607. The reconciliation of an errant father, husband, or lover with his long-suffering daughter, wife, or mistress is a strong concluding feature of most of the romances, but it's also found in various forms as early as *The Comedy of Errors*. Its universality saves us from the painful fantasy of blissful Anne Shakespeare and tearful Susanna welcoming repentant William back to the domestic hearth, so that he can get on with writing *WT*.

No, the shift to romances is a literary question calling for a literary answer, and it's with some relief that one abandons the slippery ground of psychobiography, with its plethora of maybe-questions, blue-sky analogies, and mawkish scenarios, for the firm terrain of some texts. A first stepping-stone, then, is that three of the last four plays before the romances—*Timon*, *Coriolanus*, and *Lear*—share a common characteristic: their central theme is ingratitude. In this respect they are not unique; *As You Like It*, that faraway, tinkling analogue to *Tmp.*, has a lot to say about ingratitude; so does the historical sequence from *Richard II* to *Henry V*, and likewise *Julius Caesar*. But neither the word nor the concept plays much part in the three problem comedies, so-called (*Troilus*, *All's Well*, and *Measure for Measure*); nor is ingratitude prominent in the three tragedies of *Hamlet*, *Macbeth*, and *Othello*. It is true that if one is looking deliberately for ingratitude, Iago could be called ungrateful to Othello, Macbeth to Duncan, and Claudius to Hamlet Senior; but that's not the way the stories are presented. None of the three villains is shown as having received special benefits or as owing particular loyalty to his victim. Fratricide joined with regicide is horrible enough, and Iago's black and nameless crime against Othello is ghastly enough, not to need aggravating by that particular circumstance. Coriolanus, Timon, and Lear, however, are tortured by this viper's tooth to the exclusion, almost, of all others. All three of them have, it may be, brought their troubles on themselves; it is an important element in the plays' makeup, but the hero/victims, abetted by their creator, hardly allow us to dwell on it. This is because the victim of ingratitude, who is the hero of his own story, sees his experience almost entirely from his own point of view. He is fixated on his own injuries, isolated from the world by the canker of mistrust in his mind. Stabbed to the heart by ingratitude, he sees all efforts to restore his confidence as deliberate preludes to the next act of betrayal. Half-defiant, half-pathetic, he is torn between fury at the injustice done him and shame at his impotence to wreak adequate revenge. These generalizations are made to apply to Coriolanus, Timon, and Lear; if I am correct in thinking they apply pretty well, the case is extraordinary among Shakespearean heroes. Another group of three, standing so parallel, in such important respects, would be hard to find.

Lear and *Coriolanus* can be dated, more or less, 1605 and 1607; the former at least is said to have been performed on St. Stephen's night, Christmas 1606; we don't know if or when the latter was performed, but a few of the very indefinite topical allusions are not incompatible with 1607. The more gritty and savage play *Timon of Athens* is considerably more of a mystery. The text, between verse in disarray and prose printed as verse, ill-coordinated actions, and extraordinary variations in the level of writing, has provoked more than the usual number of theories. It has been supposed an old play partly reworked by Shakespeare, a new play that he left unfinished, a play in which a collaborator took a hand, a play patched together from very foul papers indeed, and a play disturbed in the writing by various domestic catastrophes supposed to have befallen Shakespeare. Without speculating about extra-literary causes, one could assemble a substantial body of opinion in agreement that the play was abandoned in an unfinished state. The least specific reason for such abandon is likely the best; Shakespeare, it would seem, found the material "intractable." And, if one adds these several uncertainties to the fact that no record survives of a performance or of any publication before the Folio of 1623, a good presumption seems to lie that the writing of *Timon*, whenever begun, dragged on after the completion of *Lear* and *Coriolanus*. If it were in fact the last of the ingratitude plays, and an artistic failure to an extent rare if not unique in Shakespeare's literary history, this complex of events might offer some hints toward an explanation of Shakespeare's sudden shift toward the very different mode of dramatic romance.

That *Timon* includes a more deliberate and grinding demonstration of man's ingratitude than either *Lear* or *Coriolanus* is a truism that needs, I suppose, no demonstration; one after another, the friends who fed on Timon's bounty are brought on stage to make their predictable, even monotonous, excuses for not helping him in his need. Athens, which has owed its existence to Alcibiades (in the play: never mind history), brutally refuses his plea on behalf of a fellow soldier. With only one exception, Timon's servants desert like rats their master's sinking fortunes. But these actions—his compulsive generosity early in the play, his equally compulsive bitterness later—come to a climax in two closely-placed diatribes of Timon's, that beginning

> Live loathed and long,
> Most smiling, smooth, detested parasites,
> Courteous destroyers, affable wolves, meek bears
>
> (III.vi.86)

and the even more vitriolic vituperation of Athens (and by implication of the human race) that opens Act IV. After these cataclysmic denunciations, there is nowhere for Timon to go, verbally—nothing left to express. He pretends to parley with a pair of robbers, a pair of whores, and with Apemantus; but his speech always miscarries. He praises the calling of the robbers with such zest that in the end they grow ashamed of it. He incites the whores with equal violence to spread their disgusting diseases throughout Athens even as they sink, themselves, into filth and corruption; the only language they listen to is the gold he throws at them. His colloquy with Apemantus, too disagreeable almost to be read over in patience, opens with the pretentious, self-pitying question of which has most reason for his cynicism, but soon degenerates into a set of insult-slinging, root-eating, and stone-throwing contests, the last stage of which is a mere exchange of abusive monosyllables: "Beast!" "Slave!" "Toad!" "Rogue, rogue, rogue!" The two dirty old men sitting on an empty stage screaming useless epithets at one another could readily be transferred into Beckett's theater; in Shakespeare's framework they bespeak the play's disintegration and the departure of the characters to some realm outside humanity. Timon cannot even achieve the simplest final act common to us all, which is to die; it is as if he had already within his mind died to his humanity, and so need not die any further.

"Intractable" the material of *Timon* surely was; and Shakespeare's struggle to command it seems like the strongest negative impulse toward that major shift in poetic tonality and dramatic construction that actually took place in the turn to romance. Yet there are elements of positive foreshadowing as well. The first two parts of the play, with their violent alternations of Timon's mood, read almost like the comedy of humors that will be made apparent in king Leontes of *WT*; and the episodic ending, in which Alcibiades (!) unexpectedly imposes a *dénouement-de-convenance* on the play's irreconcilable differences could be thought to anticipate the peace patched together at the end of *Cym*.

But the strongest premonitions of the romances to come are found, I think, in the tragedy of *Antony and Cleopatra*. This is not just because it's "romantic" in the movie-magazine sense, but because of the way in which its characters are compounded and its narrative is constructed. Obviously, it is not a tragedy of ingratitude or betrayal, any more than of isolation; indeed, the extent to which it is a tragedy at all remains an open question. The *Liebestod* with which it concludes is an action as strong and exultant as that which ends the closet-drama of Villiers de l'Isle-Adam's post-Wagnerian *Axel*; in dying to the dungy earth, Antony and Cleopatra affirm that their love has always been imaginative, artistic, spiritual, symbolic, anything but worldly. They have been, themselves, the most worldly of lovers; but their love and the death to which it leads them transform them into something else. Antony will henceforth be such a man as Cleopatra (and behind her, Shakespeare) has imagined him, such a man as stolid Dolabella and sensible Enobarbus cannot even conceive of. Cleopatra has escaped not only the indignities of a triumph and the worse indignity of her squeaky presence on an English stage, but her own mutable nature, her own fear that she may be not a royal slut but just a slut. Each has suggested a second nature to the other; that they die voluntarily in their best identities is the highest privilege life can afford them. The sense of a man haunted by a second personality as Antony is haunted by his Genius (II.iii; IV.iv) hints at elements of *WT* where greater presences seem to lurk behind, not only the protagonists but some of the minor persons as well.

Not only does *Antony* end triumphantly as well as tragically, it is constructed like a romance, more episodically than inevitably. Until the last minute we cannot be sure that Antony will not beg mercy of Caesar (for a moment, in III.xii, he actually does so); there is hardly a moment before the last when Cleopatra is not capable of turning into a flincher. The play deliberately cultivates that sort of uncertainty. With dozens of different locales, from Syria to Athens, Actium, Alexandria, Misenum, Messina, and Rome, the action reels around the Mediterranean, as if to bewilder the audience even further. What the play does not have, to qualify it as a proper romance, is a variety of social levels and dialects, a sense of strangeness and adventure. It takes place on a stage of public action, and prevailingly in the heroic idiom. So it does not directly foreshadow the romance plots, and from *Antony* one could no more anticipate the coming of *Per.* or *WT* than from *Timon*. Still, these two tragedies can be considered swings of the pendulum in the last stage of Shakespeare's career as a writer of the heroic, the egotistical sublime.

Apart from the dimensions of the central characters, and the extent to which the play focusses on their feelings, the romances seem to be feminized to a much greater degree than plays like *Timon* and *Coriolanus*. Less gusty and gutsy than the Roman general and his Egyptian queen, the romance heroes find in their heroines forces of spiritual redemption—indeed, on the common level of sexual attraction, the girls are often taboo. As in the poems of T. S. Eliot and Ezra Pound, sex may be omnipresent but it is generally distanced, like a natural force strained through the learned pages of Sir J. G. Frazer, rather than a zesty relation between people. Rare is the commentator who takes with full seriousness the notion of erotic contact between Miranda and Ferdinand, the attraction of Imogen to Posthumus, the commitment of Perdita to Florizel, or the perfunctory contract between Marina and Lysimachus. Marriages seal the social bond, reform the family ties, bode well for the burgeoning future; they may even offer to those in need of it a kind of moral redemption, not specifically Christian but perfectly compatible with practical Christianity. Perhaps because they cannot be felt on the human level as strong erotic experiences, symbolic and semi-religious meanings have clustered naturally around these hushed and reverent unions. How much of this mythological or mythical, but generally rhetorical, nimbus is legitimately attached to the romances depends so largely on the original prepossessions of the reader that the question will never be decided once and for all. But that this sort of material gravitates more liberally toward the romances than toward other Shakespeare plays is a potent index of their character.

If only because they are comedies of a sort—a sort structurally and tonally distinct from the earlier "romantic comedies"—the romances operate at a lower and a more diffused level of psychic tension than the immediately preceding tragedies. (Romances tend to string out on a line the adventures of the hero striving toward his remote goal, while both comedies and tragedies take a shorter perspective, and concentrate. Romances stretch out (in some of their early forms,

interminably, i.e., as long as the audience wanted some
more); the force of tragedies and comedies is centripetal,
concentrative, and so better adapted to the limited time and
space of the stage.) Each of Shakespeare's romances contains
a moment, sometimes a relaxed and extended moment, of
the semi-relevant idyllic; lyrical descriptions of flowers and
rural ceremonies are scattered like bouquets, one notable
passage to a play. Of a piece with this new emphasis on
charm is a persistent concern with innocence and (in three
of the four plays) specifically with chastity. Judging not simply by the calendar but by the impression they make on
stage, the lovers whose union resolves a Shakespeare romance are often adolescent children. Partly this is a result
of the playwright's perspective, in looking on his characters
from above and afar as elements of a pattern; it is also in
part a romance convention. Since the scenic, sentimental
adventures of Daphnis and Chloe, the wanderings of milk-
white innocents through a world of menace have provided
a common theme of romantic adventure; Shakespeare could
have been drawn to the formula by contrast with the case-
hardened, inflexible heroes of his most recent tragedies. The
scene for his romance-adventures is set not only in remote
locales but often in mysterious, undefined antiquity. Under
these circumstances improbabilities become less improbable,
and a dramatist with a sense of humor can introduce deliberate anachronisms like Boult the bawdy-house bouncer, Autolycus the roadside prig, and Posthumus' sardonic, knowing
gaoler.

These points of differentiation could be multiplied almost
indefinitely; most point to a contrast with the antecedent
tragedies, a reaction. Elements of positive inspiration seem
to derive from the comedies, particularly *As You Like It*. (The
mysterious magician with whom Rosalind mystifies Orlando
in Act V—he is said to be her uncle, and to live "obscuréd
in the circle of this forest"—sounds like a remote anticipation

of Prospero.) But apart from particular influences, Shakespeare's romances all fall within that mysterious, half-defined country which cannot be limited, only explored—the world of quest and conflict, of erotic and religious seeking, of chivalric and pastoral adventure which is to this day an open frontier of story. Outside the round of theater, romantic narrative had many applications over a long history. It was in effect the main stream of popular narrative, but it overflowed those banks in many different directions. And therein lies a problem.

For a romance may display so many different qualities that definition is impossible and even examples confuse more than they illuminate. Quest is near the heart of the concept—an attempt at recovery or discovery that leads the displaced person past obstacles and distractions (sometimes, alas, over *longueurs* in the narrative) to his place of rest. Examples range from "The Hunting of the Snark" to the Christian epic, from the legend of the Grail to "Rasselas." Romance is compatible with epic or dramatic form, with ballads, burlesques, histories, operas, beast fables, moralities, saints' lives, sagas, motions, coffeehouse stories, lais, fabliaux, and every conceivable form of prose narrative. In structure a romance tends to be more episodic than close-knit; it is more likely to follow an individual than explore a group; its protagonist is likely to encounter a great variety of human types scattered across a wide range of places and a great expanse of time. Accident, coincidence, and arbitrary changes of intention resolve the action more often than does the inexorable working out of a plot. Elementary probability may be disregarded, wonders invoked. Nobody of prime importance will ordinarily be killed, but the protagonist undergoes many tribulations—often long-drawn-out, because the nature of romance is extensive—before reaching his end. Since no romance shows every one of these characteristics, and many narratives which are not primarily romances show some of them, the outlines of the term are nebulous in the extreme. Tinges of romance are just about everywhere; and in every romance (except possibly the very silliest) there is a streak of hard realism, a blunt bit of fact that directly counters the fantasy or even Boojums the quest itself.

Because we don't know what we're talking about, it's quite impossible to say how much of the semi-romance, pseudo-romance, romance-tinged literature Shakespeare was acquainted with, except that it must have been an immense lot. Shades and traces of romance-feeling go back to his very first work for the stage. On the other hand, none of those earlier plays has ever been identified as belonging in any of the formal traditions of romance writing. *As You Like It* took its plot from Lodge's *Rosalynde*, for which we have no other word than a Euphuistic romance; yet there has been no effort to take it out of the other comedies—*Twelfth Night, Much Ado, All's Well*—and judge it by a different standard. The early comedies, with their court-intrigues, contrived misunderstandings, wit-combats, and formal pairings-off, belong to a different world from the later romances. It may be only a matter of quantity; they show fewer of the qualities of the romance proper, more of the qualities of a love-game played for its own sake. The conclusion of all is that though he knew many romances, and had used many of their elements in previous plays, Shakespeare when he turned to writing the four plays starting with *Per.* faced a problem that was new and different, in degree if not in kind. The precedents on which he could rely for stage-writing in that new mode were neither many nor impressive; the problems of episodic structure on a constricted stage, of characters less than totally absorbent of audience-sympathy, were formidable. Early on, he had been able to follow well-established precedent in courtship comedies, heroic tragedies, even moralized English histories; but in the new mode of stage romance he had to feel his way with some hesitations and the occasional misstep. In the scaffolding held up by Gower, in Leontes' jealousy, in the misogynistic rant of Posthumus, it's possible to see that the transition was not only slow but hard.

So far as feasible, it's probably better to explain literary consequences in terms of literary causes. But, if only for completeness, some of the other theories should be mentioned. The more extreme biographical guesses—as that Shakespeare experienced a nervous breakdown, a religious conversion, or a life crisis provoked by the death of his brother in 1607—have been asked to explain many different phenomena, and have served one occasion about as well as another. The notion that Shakespeare in taking up romances was following the lead of Beaumont and Fletcher trips over obstinate chronology: *Per.* had to be written no later than the first months of 1608, *Philaster* cannot possibly be moved back far enough to constitute an influence. Besides, Shakespeare as an established playwright would be more likely to influence than to follow a pair of neophytes. Access to the Blackfriars theater also postdates the writing of *Per.*; and the King's Men did not have to have plays written to order for every fresh venue where they performed. It's a minor detail that two and perhaps three of the romances are known to have been performed at the Globe, none (that we know of) at the Blackfriars. In any event, these proposed causes seem woefully inadequate to account for the known consequences.

On another level entirely, it has been proposed that Shakespeare in his final period was completing on a life-large scale a kind of tragic pattern, defined as prosperity–destruction–re-creation which he had previously adumbrated in other plays but here brought to triumphant completion. The romances are the re-creation stage of the total dramatic pattern, in which the poet gave symbolic expression to his culminating vision of life. This implies an impressive degree of foresight or confidence on Shakespeare's part, since three of the four romances were not printed till seven years after the poet's death, and the other one (*Per.*) is little better than a textual mess. In addition, there is no evidence anywhere that Shakespeare intended his plays to be studied for a pattern woven into their total architecture. If he had taken a textual scholar's view of his work, he might well have used his last years at Stratford to straighten out some of the bibliographical problems and interpretive cruxes that have vexed the last four centuries. On the evidence, nothing was further from his thoughts—except perhaps the fantasy of an overarching psychic message woven into the fabric of his entire theatrical production, or a cipher enabling us to discover that "Francis Bacon wrote this play."

In exactly the opposite direction, commentary has surmised that the various, almost fragmentary character of the romances may possess profound expressive value; it shows the playwright standing awestruck before the bewildering variety and complexity of the Creator's many levels of earthly reality. Perhaps the chief difficulty with this view is that it constitutes an argument against writing anything at all, let alone a stage play with a silly little story. Faced with the full complexity and beauty of the universe, one probably shouldn't try to improve on the most vulgar of modern formulas: "Oooh, wow!" is only imperceptibly more inadequate than Shelley's "Hymn to Intellectual Beauty." But that Shakespeare ever asked the players of the King's Company to render such breathless ecstasy on a London stage while simultaneously amusing the public with clowns, bumpkins, and pretty boys made up as princesses, we're entitled to doubt.

The smaller the problem, the less of a solution is called for. Just conceivably Shakespeare did not sit down and say,

"I have encountered a life-crisis; what I must do now is write a set of four romances." *Timon*, there's no question about it, is the work of a dramatist in artistic trouble; and just about that time, a script titled "Apollonius" or "Pericles" turned up on the playwright's desk, or (more likely) backstage at the Globe. Somebody—whether George Wilkins or another—had picked up the story in one of its several versions, and worked on the first two acts of a play. Wilkins demands consideration because we know he had an interest in the story, because one of his own plays had already been put on by the King's Men—and because of the quality of that play. Anyone who has dipped into *The Miseries of Enforced Marriage* will see at once how inadequate Wilkins must have felt before a script calling for real poetry. Perhaps first, perhaps last, he turned to Shakespeare—who, as a man of living imagination, found something in the story that attracted him, as a man of the theater found in the play some problems, incompletely solved, that bothered him, and as a man of business found that this mouldy, patched-up script held the attention of audiences. "What can we do with *this*?"—it's a question that rises in the mind of every craftsman who finds in his hands something a little out of the way. As he works into his materials, paths open before him. His second venture is better than his first, and his third much better than either.

Maybe that is how it happened. Though it's only a guess, it's far from the most pointless of available guesses. What's for sure is that the four romances comprise a discrete group though not an organic one; compared with each other, they are very different, though contrasted with Shakespeare's other plays they have important points in common. A recent production by Peter Hall for the National Theater of Britain (encompassing three of the four plays, *Per.* omitted) was able, so I'm told, to suggest this balance of unity in diversity by having the same actor take analogous roles in different plays.

It seems like a neat, cogent way to make a major critical point, silently.

REFERENCES

Derek M. Traversi, *Shakespeare the Last Phase* (London, 1954) relies heavily on plot paraphrase, but points toward a loose Christian view of the romances which after a while waters down to "a balanced view of life."

Shakespeare's Last Plays by E. M. W. Tillyard (Humanities Press, 1983) rose out of a set of lectures delivered in 1936; bypassing *Per.*, it proposes that the other three romances develop and complete patterns adumbrated in the earlier tragedies but not completed there.

Philip Edwards' survey, "Shakespeare's Romances 1900–1957" appeared in *Shakespeare Survey* 11 (1958); it provides an early, if not the first, strong questioning of the symbolic interpretations that blossomed so luxuriantly after WW II. Edwards is not a basher of allegorical or symbolic approaches; but he provides strong reasons for handling them cautiously. A similar retrospect by F. David Hoeniger in *Shakespeare Survey* 29 (1976) updates the major areas of discussion, though in a less decisive way than Edwards.

The symbolic interpretations of G. Wilson Knight, as they aim to chart the dramatist's spiritual development (*Myth and Miracle*, 1929; *The Crown of Life*, 1948), emphasize spheres of racial wisdom and unchanging fundamental verities to which a text-bound reader finds it hard to attune.

Alfred Harbage, in *Shakespeare and the Rival Traditions* (New York, 1952), stresses the differences between the popular theater, for which Shakespeare prevailingly wrote, and the courtly or coterie mode, to which he vigorously denies the last plays were addicted.

E. C. Pettet, *Shakespeare and the Romance Tradition* (Staples Press, 1947), urges the importance of Sidney's *Arcadia* and the long line of idyllic narratives in which it stands, not only to Shakespeare's last plays but to the much earlier "romantic" comedies.

Frances Yates, *Shakespeare's Last Plays* (London, 1975), tries to tie some of them to court factions and royal politics, through comparison with some of the court masques. If they made the plays more interesting, instead of duller, the arguments (learned and detailed as usual with Ms. Yates) might be more persuasive.

Clifford Leech argues in "The Structure of the Last Plays," *Shakespeare Survey* 11 (1958), that a tightly articulated five-act pattern, not very apparent in *Per.* and *Cym.* (which rely heavily on coincidence and accident), is more evident in *WT* and *Tmp.*

Howard W. Felperin, *Shakespearean Romance* (Princeton, 1972), provides a recondite, frequently brilliant, and always well-written account of the plays and their background; but his book, centering on the slippery and elusive word "romance," and stretching it across the centuries, grants the word (I think) too much liberty to assume whatever meaning it chooses.

L. C. Knights, "On Historical Scholarship and the Interpretation of Shakespeare," *Sewanee Review* LXIII no. 2 (Spring, 1955) mediates suggestively and sensitively between those who try to recover what Shakespeare meant to audiences of his day and those who try to impose on him an extravagant range of modern meanings.

In *A Natural Perspective* (1965) Northrop Frye lays such weight on the "principles of dramatic structure" as the central interest of the romances that the approach threatens to reduce the plays to skeletons or stencils. Fortunately the principles are not only largely undefined (so that each play seems to have its own admirable and sufficient principles) but all principles are subsumed by an appeal to "myth," which suffuses formulas that might seem abstract with its own ineffable glow.

Of books titled simply *Shakespeare*, a preliminary accounting would include those by Edward Dowden (1875), A. C. Swinburne (1905), J. M. Murry (1906), Walter Raleigh (1907), Mark Van Doren (1941), Ivor Brown (1949), and Allardyce Nicoll (1952).

More detailed studies, dating from before 1950, listed alphabetically, and including only those of particular potential interest to readers of this study, are:

- Armstrong, E. A., *Shakespeare's Imagination* (1946)
- Brandes, Georg, *William Shakespeare a Critical Study* (1899)
- Chambers, E. K., *The Elizabethan Stage* (4 volumes, 1923)

- Ellis-Fermor, Una, *The Jacobean Drama* (1947)
- Harbage, Alfred, *Shakespeare's Audience* (1941)
- Partridge, Eric, *Shakespeare's Bawdy* (1947)
- Pettet, E. C., *Shakespeare and the Romance Tradition* (1949)
- Saintsbury, George, *The Flourishing of Romance and the Rise of Allegory* (1897)
- *Shakespeare's England* (2 volumes, 1926)
- Sisson, C. J., *The Mythical Sorrows of Shakespeare* (1934)
- Spencer, Theodore, *Shakespeare and the Nature of Man* (1942)
- Wilson, F. P., *Elizabethan and Jacobean* (1945)

Since 1948 the *Shakespeare Survey* and since 1950 the *Shakespeare Quarterly* have provided bibliographical help in keeping up with the spate of commentary.

II

PERICLES

THE FOLK-STORY THAT WOULD EVENTUALLY TAKE SHAPE AS *Pericles Prince of Tyre* originated somewhere in the eastern Mediterranean at a remote and indefinite period of time. Probably it was first written in Greek, like the third-century (A.D.) romances of Heliodorus, Longus, and Achilles Tatius, but nothing is known of the original form of the tale, or of its author if it had one. It may have begun as several stories of communal authorship; the earliest manuscript we have is in Latin, and dates from the 8th or 9th century A.D.—that is, by the roughest of estimates, more than a thousand years from the time the fable started wandering from teller to listener around the marketplaces of the Levant. In all early texts, the hero's name is Apollonius, that of his daughter Tarsia or some variant thereof; but the broad outline of the plot is substantially that of the play as we have it. The wanderings of Tarsia during her long separation from Apollonius were embellished with various episodes, and a number of extraneous but apparently amusing conundrums were added to the scene where father and daughter are reunited. But the narrative held its shape surprisingly. The preliminary story of Antiochus, his daughter, and the fateful riddle that every suitor must answer was awkwardly stuck on the front of the main narrative some time in its early history; it still maintains only a precarious connection; yet it never came unstuck.* As over a hundred manuscript copies survive, the legend of Apollonius must have been widely popular. It can be surmised—but only surmised—that its episodic structure, its exotic setting, its sensational reverses of fortune, and the strong pathos of the hero's undeserved suffering contributed to its popular acceptance. Apollonius, though born a prince, has to recover through patience and fortitude his true inheritance, his rightful family, his position in the world. It is a theme that foreshadows a lot of English fiction (dozens of examples will present themselves), and apparently worked just as well in the middle ages.

The folklore character of "Apollonius of Tyre" may have been one reason why it was preserved, almost unchanged, across the centuries; though a random, helter-skelter narration, it was formulaic. Most transcribers of it copied, more or less accurately, the version placed before them; they had no aspirations to make more of the story than it had made of itself. In the 13th century, Chaucer's friend John Gower ("the moral Gower") picked up Apollonius for inclusion in his poetical compendium, *Confessio Amantis*. This is a collection of narratives through which Genius, a priest of Venus, provides guidance for the conscience of a lover, Amans. The stories are arranged to illustrate the Seven Deadly Sins, and the story of Apollonius is supposed to illustrate lust. This is achieved by making the chastity of Tarsia, who after many wanderings and misfortunes achieves happiness, contrast with the wretched end of Antiochus' nameless daughter,

---

* The romance contains one small bit of semi-historical fact; according to II Maccabees 9, Antiochus IV did suffer the horrid fate of the character in the play. He suffered, however, not for incest, but for cruelty to the Chosen People.

cruelly punished with her father for the sin of incest. Chaucer's Man of Law in his prologue voiced distaste for the incest theme, and though the point cannot be proved was probably alluding to Gower's handling of it.

A detail such as the riddle that must be solved to win Antiochus' daughter can illustrate the closeness with which Gower followed the legend and *Pericles* the play followed Gower:

Legend	Gower	Pericles
Scelere vehor.	With felonie I am upbore,	I am no viper, yet I feed
Materna carne vescor.	I ete and have it noght forbore	On mother's flesh, which did me breed.
Quero patrem meum	Mi modres fleissh, whos housebond	I sought a husband, in which labor
Matris mee virum	Mi fader for to seche I fonde,	I found that kindness in a father.
Uxoris mee filiam	Which is the Sone eke of my wif.	He's father, son, and husband mild,
Nec invenio.	Hierof I am inquisitif;	I mother, wife, and yet his child.
	And who that can mi tale save,	How they may be, and yet in two
	Al quyt he schal my doghter have	As you will live, resolve it you.
	Of his ansuere and if he fail	
	He schal be ded withoute faile.	

(I.i.65 ff.)

The parallelism here is exceptionally close, as in only one other passage of equivalent length (the letter enclosed in Thaisa's "coffin"), but it shows careful attention to Gower. Other parallels are less extensive, and mostly the play paraphrases Gower without following him verbally. In the first two scenes of Act II and in Act IV, scene iii (the dispute between Dionyza and Cleon) the play presents material for which there is no warrant in Gower. But these are exceptions; the general rule is that, compared with *Cym.* or *WT*, *Per.* adheres to its major source with notable fidelity. The fact stands out because Apollonius' legend is really too sprawling to lend itself to stage presentation. It makes an outsize play. We have records of a 1619 occasion when the performance had to stop for refreshments after the first two acts, and then continued till two A.M. Probably this was because, between Gower's explanations, frequent dumb-shows, and an actual performance, the same material may be presented three times over.

Though slight individually, these anomalies may point toward a special problem with *Per.*, going beyond slipshod reporting or careless compositors. And the ramifications of this problem must be my excuse for a discussion of the text of *Per.* more extensive than will be required for any of the other romances.

Though Gower was the primary source through whom the Apollonius legend reached the Globe theater, he was hardly the only one. A version in English prose by one Lawrence Twine was probably published in 1576 and definitely printed or reprinted in 1594 and 1607; it was a translation of a French version of the 153d story in the *Gesta Romanorum*, and was titled *The Pattern of Painful Adventures*. For a couple of scenes in Act IV, *Per.* follows closely the version of the story as presented by Twine, and departs from Gower. It is not impossible that the Latin text of the *Gesta Romanorum* was itself laid under minor contribution; and some other retellings of the old story may have been available, but their possible influences on the play are too dubious to merit much attention.

Between them, Gower and Twine account for a very large part of *Per.*'s story line, and some of the phrasing as well; whoever wrote it up knew both of them. And so the play was produced; we know where and pretty well when. The 1609 Quarto is explicit about the place: "as it hath been divers and sundry times acted by his Majesty's Servants at the Globe on the Bank-side," and the date is set by independent testimony of the Venetian ambassador who saw the play performed late in 1607 or 1608. But during its composition, and on its way from the playhouse to the 1609 Quarto text, *Per.* suffered a set of major mutilations. Most tangible is the damage done by the compositors who, in addition to printing a good deal of utter nonsense and mislabelling many speeches, were baffled by the problems of blank verse and either reduced it to tatters or printed it as prose. They also made stage characters understand and react to decisions of other stage characters before they had been made. Beyond the compositors lie the reporters who tried to assemble a script from their confused and faulty recollections of the play. Their presence is revealed by a pattern of repetitions resulting from memorial contamination of one passage by words from another, and by a set of stage-directions that marches actors onstage for no reason and then marches them off again without a word said. And then, even before reporters and compositors got their blundering fingers on it, the play-text seems to have been confused by two authors at least, who tried to patch together a coherent drama out of antecedent materials from Gower and Twine.

One of these authors, it is generally supposed, was William Shakespeare. The play was published under his name within a year or two of its production; nobody directly challenged his authorship, and though the compilers of the First Folio did not endorse the attribution, their failure to include the play could have had a number of causes.* Shakespeare was the leading playwright for "his Majesty's Servants," i.e., the King's Men. That he had a part in the script is more than probable, it is practically certain. As for the other author, or in this case compiler, a number of candidates have been proposed, but as the case for all of them but one rests on internal evidence, it makes sense to look first at the lone exception. This is a journeyman author—playwright, journalist, pamphleteer—named George Wilkins. In 1608, the year before the Quarto appeared, he brought forth with a different publisher a book titled *The Painful Adventures of Pericles Prince of Tyre*. The titlepage of this prose narrative raises an elusive and evasive signpost. On the one hand it specifically claims to be "the true history of the play of Pericles, as it was lately presented by the worthy and ancient poet John Gower"; and a woodcut below presents the image of Gower himself. This emphasis on Gower is at odds with the book's contents, for two reasons. Wilkins never mentions Gower in his own text. Where he copies from anyone, it is from Twine, on whose version of the Pericles/Apollonius story he relies, moderately at first but later on very heavily indeed (as, presumably, he got bored or tired). And, most obviously, by making Gower the "presenter" of the play, he blocks out all mention of Shakespeare. These are indirections, if not dishonesties. But there is another side to this clearly shabby man. In several passages occurring during the last

* They may have felt the only texts available to them were too corrupt; they may have had doubts about the copyright; they may have been reluctant to print any play not entirely by Shakespeare (they omitted *The Two Noble Kinsmen*); or, having had troubles with the text of *Timon*, they may not have wanted any more grief.

three acts of the play (the part commonly assigned to Shakespeare) he gives fuller versions of passages which the Quarto
represents very inadequately. Some scholars have suggested
that there was an earlier play called *Pericles* (an Ur-*Pericles*,
so to speak) from which both the scrappy play-text and Wilkins' prose narrative derive. But this is multiplying essences
praeter necessitatem; the internal evidence for Wilkins as co-
author of *Per.* is just as strong as for anyone else; his knowledge of the play is in places better than that of the bumbling
reporters who furnished such wretched copy for the bumbling compositors:* what stands against his election to the
post of co-author? A very striking phrase in the dedication
of his *Painful Adventures* (to Maister Henry Fermor, J.P. for
Middlesex) makes *for* his participation in the play while intimating that the circumstances of that arrangement were
less than happy. "I see, Sir," says the distressed author,
"that a good coat with rich trappings gets a gay ass entrance
in at a great gate (and within a may stalk freely) when a
ragged philosopher with more wit shall be shut forth of
doors." This phrase of jealous pique fits well with the portrait
of Gower on the title page which so effactually blocks out
the name of Shakespeare in connection with the play while
at the same time enabling Wilkins to hang on the coat-tails

---

* Everyone involved in production of the Quarto play and George Wilkins'
Painful Adventures stood a little below the threshold of publishing respectability. A reputable publisher, Edward Blount, did indeed register
what may have been a good copy of the play on May 20, 1608, but he
never proceeded further with it. Instead, a man named Henry Gosson,
who had never before published a play, got hold of the copy, probably
surreptitiously, and shared out the printing of it with a couple of other
shops. Wilkins' publisher was a man named Thomas Purfoot.

The new Oxford Shakespeare (1986) offers a reconstructed text of *Per.*,
melding the Folio text with Wilkins' novel and specifying joint authorship;
on the other hand, Sina Spiker in an extended study of the play's authorship (*SP* XXX, 1933, pp. 551 ff.) concludes that Wilkins had no hand
in writing it. The matter is far from positive resolution.

of the drama. Put these details together with the common consensus that the first two acts of the play passed a different process than the last three, and one has the makings of a prudent theory.

To put it briefly: the 1607 republication of Twine's book called attention to the old Apollonius-legend; Wilkins, on the prowl for material, picked it up and enlisted help to make it a drama (on one of his two previous dramatic efforts, he had already collaborated)—turning, when work on the script had reached about the end of Act II, to Shakespeare. For reasons that have to be guessed, Shakespeare was attracted to the script, perhaps did some patching work on the first two acts, but found it easier to write the last three himself than to tow in his wake a prosaic collaborator or set of collaborators. Wilkins, without the gift of dramatic construction or poetic invention but not a wholly untalented scribbler, was wounded at being supplanted by a more gifted and confident writer; his prose fiction was an effort to assert his own impugned talents, to pre-empt publication of the play script when and if it should take place, and to make a bit of money from an idea that he considered "his." He may even have been successful to the extent of discouraging Edward Blount from going ahead with publication, thereby leaving *Per.* to the scratched-up, makeshift procedures of Henry Gosson *et al.*

A major objection to this reconstruction is that Wilkins, though elsewhere a consistent plagiarist, does not in his prose tale copy closely the first two acts of *Per.* the play, for which he was (according to the scenario) responsible; given his penchant for transcribing, it does not seem likely that he would scruple to imitate himself. This might be a fair objection if Wilkins were thought to have written the first two acts of *Per.* alone and unaided. But he has recently been offered a collaborator in the person of John Day, who had

worked with him on another play, *Law Tricks*.* Day was a
practiced poet; Wilkins' only unaided play (*The Miseries of
Enforced Marriage*) moves on the ground level of prose at its
most prosaic. Though the King's Men had staged *The Miseries*, Wilkins could hardly have failed to see that he would
need a lot of help to make anything stageworthy out of the
Apollonius legend. Had he associated Day with himself in
the composition of *Per.*'s first acts, that might account both
for the text of those acts (improved well above the level of
The Miseries) and for Wilkins' reluctance to copy that text in
his "novel," because Day was alive, present, and potentially
vocal. Copying from Twine, who had copied from the French
translator of the *Gesta Romanorum*, and who by 1607 was
probably dead, certainly obscure, was much safer. In fact,
we cannot lightly assume that Wilkins on his own (i.e., before
the writing of the play), knew anything whatever about
Gower. The last previous edition of *Confessio Amantis* (1554)
had been more than fifty years before; and Wilkins, no
scholar, tended to pick occasions for his writing from the
flotsam of current journalism and current events. Quite possibly in the first drafts of the play's first acts Gower was not
present at all, as he is not present in Wilkins' *Painful
Adventures*.

Suppose, then, Shakespeare facing the trunk of a fairly ill-
composed play, encompassing the story of Apollonius' per-
ilous adventures at Antioch, his return to Tyre, his flight
from the assassin, his bringing timely supply to Tarsus, his
shipwreck near Pentapolis, his participation in the tournament, his winning of Thaisa, and his receipt of word from
Tyre that it is now safe to come home. Act III enters, almost
like a new play, on the story of Pericles' wife and daughter,
the apparent death, rebirth, and long sequestration of Thaisa,

---

* F. D. Hoeniger, ed., *Pericles* (Arden edition), Appendix B. See also *Shakespeare Quarterly* XI (1960), 27.

the several perils of Marina, the long separation of the family, and their final happy reunion, beyond all hope. One can understand the trepidation of the original author or authors in embarking on this second story; it involves another storm at sea, an apparent resurrection, the testing under extreme circumstances of a virgin endowed with sacred eloquence, and a father-daughter recognition scene requiring a very delicate hand. The comparatively external maneuvers and practical responses of the first part of the play would have to give way in the second part to heightened eloquence, a sense of mystery, and a richer poetry, if the impossible were to be made credible and the merely exotic humanly moving. For help, they turned to a practiced playwright and the best poet available; but what did he see in the script that attracted him?

He saw a story remote in space and distant in time; those being the conditions of it, the presence of Gower, whether he had been present in the first two acts as originally sketched or not, could only be a good thing. The archaisms of Gower's speech would create a sense of deep antiquity, while the characters of the play need not use an ancient dialect that, cumulatively, would become irksome and laborious. (Note that the author, through Gower, betrays some uneasiness, in the Chorus before IV.iv, that in all the many places represented on stage, everyone speaks the same English.) Equally useful along the same lines was the tournament at Pentapolis; it blurred medieval with Hellenistic and even some Old Testament overtones in the play, and extended the note of riddling and puzzling already present in the Antiochus story by displaying a pageant of knightly impresas with their allegorical explanations. The range of strong scenes, from the second storm at sea to the greasy corruption of a Mytelene whorehouse promised a series of powerful dramatic opportunities. The ramshackle plot combined with the fact that this is an ancient tale, a fable out of the long ago, to relieve the pressures of quotidian realism; without being too serious about itself, the play could be half a parable.

The central figure of the *Per.* story is an old man redeemed; in various forms this personage occupies a central position in so many of the late plays that it may be presumed to have held some particular interest for Shakespeare. In the course of the play, Pericles goes out of his way to age from the gallant young suitor and bold knight-errant of Acts I and II to the shaggy, listless, almost catatonic personage of the last act. Particularly notable is his vow in III.iii to let his hair grow "unscissored," until the infant Marina shall be married. Pericles, when he makes the vow, is on his way to Tyre to resume his kingdom; assume him to be right that little Marina cannot accompany him immediately; how can he foresee that she will not join him, having been sent or fetched to Tyre, within a reasonable period of time, rather than the fourteen years she lingers in Tarsus? (By sea, the two cities are only a couple of hundred miles apart. Of course, Antioch lies between; but when Pericles leaves Marina in Tarsus, his enemy Antiochus is already dead.) In any case, why shun the barber all those years? This is a strong touch on stage, far stronger than in a narrative, where it is soon said and done. At a first level, the form of the vow (not to cut his hair till Marina is married) will be perceived as a screen for Pericles' grief at the drowning of Thaisa, his new wife. But beyond that, Shakespeare may have wanted him marked as a wanderer and an outcast, a man pursued by the enmity of the gods. (That enmity could be understood as reaching back to, or even before, the first scene of the play, when answering Antiochus' riddle was just as dangerous to Pericles' life as not answering it.) Within the motion of the play, a shaggy Pericles in Act V, scene i makes for a powerful scene, obviating all need for the costume sackcloth with which imaginative editors have cumbered the setting. In addition, his hair will provide impressive evidence for Pericles' long-continued pariah status. Though Gower tells the audience he returned to Tyre at the end of Act III, "welcomed and settled to his own desire," the audience never sees him thus complacent; without actually saying so, his unshorn locks in Act V convey an impression of lasting exile, solitary suffering, and spiritual drift. To borrow a phrase of Milton, he is "by himself given o'er."

This self-exiled wanderer was doubtless of interest to Shakespeare for his own dramatic sake; he also became the center of a drama that recurs perhaps too often in the last plays, his redemption worked out by a restored wife and a devoted daughter. This may be a story too familiar to be worth insisting on, but its very recurrence indicates its interest to the playwright; and it seems to have been here, in the old story of Apollonius, that he first glimpsed its possibilities. A special overtone involves the name of the heroine, Marina. She had been Tharsia or Thaise until Shakespeare, speaking through Pericles in III,iii,10, gave her the name of Marina, because she was born at sea. And this is like a small red flag, to which scholarship has been duly attentive, signalling that Shakespeare in this play is very conscious of the sea, very aware of the play's constant interaction with the waters of the ocean, and perhaps attracted to the old narrative because of certain effects, both dramatic and poetic, which that setting would make possible.

Documenting the details is unnecessary; to describe the various roles played by the sea in *Per.* would be practically to summarize the plot. The four major voyages of Apollonius/ Pericles were all in the story as Gower and Twine delivered it; and these the play has duly, and in good part perfunctorily, recorded. Where a vision of the sea seems to have stirred the playwright most deeply is in the storm that overtakes Pericles and his family at the beginning of Act III. In the midst of this storm Marina is born, even as Thaisa dies and is buried in the waves—only to be reborn later through the magic of Cerimon. Pericles' elegy over the body of Thaisa, beginning "A terrible childbed hast thou had, my dear," is one of the deep imaginative moments of the play. He sees himself committing her to the ooze,

> Where for a monument upon thy bones
> And e'er-remaining lamps, the belching whale
> And humming water must o'erwhelm thy corpse
> Lying with simple shells.
>
> (III.i.56 ff.)

It is a double movement that these few lines trace. As the body sinks out of air and light into the level of monsters, then into the dark of waters vibrant with invisible pressures, and finally to the bare, dead shells of the bottom, so it is stripped of sight, of hearing, and finally of sentience itself. Here Shakespeare is touching on one of the two major symbolic aspects of the ocean: it is the ultimate graveyard of identity, as well as the first source of animate life. In the Act V reunion with Marina, Pericles recalls with a father's ecstasy and a conscious artist's pointed concision that in restoring him to life, Marina is one

> that beget'st him that did thee beget,
> Thou that wast born at sea, buried at Tarsus,
> And found at sea again.
>
> (V.i.196 ff.)

The idea that in metaphor she gives birth to her own father may perhaps ring a little uncomfortably on the ear of the listener who still recalls the domestic intricacies of Antiochus' riddle; Lysimachus, only recently a patron of the town brothel, must be introduced as a screen between father and daughter, and so he is, with almost record dexterity. As for the claim of the verse that Marina was "found at sea again," that too is a little factitious; she was found in the town of Mytilene, which is a seaport like all the other towns in the play. Still, the poet's emphasis on the sea as the restoring element is only made more emphatic by this "inaccuracy"; in the same way, the profound mystery of the sea as devouring gulf is not impaired by the fact that Thaisa is not really dead. The sea is both grave and womb; it can also be, without metaphoric strain, a road beset with difficulties of which violent, treacherous storms, no less than violent, treacherous pirates, are evidence. Pericles, like Paul, whose tempestuous voyage to Italy lingers a long way in the background, must pass through storms and perils on his way to rebirth through his daughter, recovery of his wife, and restoration to his kingdoms—for he becomes monarch of Pentapolis as well as Tyre.

"Typical" or at least remote influences, intimated rather than exhibited, pervade the life story of Pericles. Diana, classical patroness of female chastity, is invoked by Thaisa in the moment of her revival and by Marina as she is dragged off to the brothel, yet she plays no apparent part in either action. The temple of Diana shelters Thaisa in Ephesus for the fourteen years of her separation from Pericles (Gower evidently conceives of it as a nunnery, and in his version Thaisa becomes the "Abbesse" of it), but her timely appearance to guide the wandering prince to Ephesus is quite arbitrary; she might have intervened any time earlier to cut short the 14-year separation, and might better have appeared to either of her two votaresses than to the hero, who has never uttered her name or given her a thought. Neither in Gower's version, in Twine's, nor in Wilkins' prose narrative does she appear to Pericles/Apollonius as a monitory vision; he has a dream, but not of Diana. And setting aside this one direct intervention of hers, which might have been a mere casting-convenience.* Diana's action in the play, though by no means unimportant, works more often atmospherically and by indirection than through participatory action. The goddess of chastity cannot be insignificant in a play the most powerful scenes of which focus on a weak and solitary girl's resistance, as star boarder in a whorehouse, against a city full of unprincipled lechers. But her action there cannot well be represented; as a principle concealed in Marina's mind, she has to allow her devotee free agency. Though elsewhere Marina is identified with "argentine" Diana by her "silver livery," the princess in the hour of crisis must be herself and stand her test alone.

Cerimon, medical mage of Ephesus, also exercises on the action the most direct of influences, by bringing back Thaisa from the dead; but, like Diana, he is impressive by virtue of the aura that surrounds him, the power he diffuses from the mythic past. The name has been taken to suggest "ceremony," but as it is not of Shakespeare's invention, no great significance need be assigned to it. No more can the poet's art be held responsible for his residence at Ephesus, a city which in the early days of the legend and even for Elizabethan readers of Acts 19, carried automatic implications of occult knowledge. A mage in a landscape of mages, Cerimon exercises the familiar yet mysterious craft of "Nature's secretary," a practitioner of hidden knowledge. In the preliminary, preparatory dialogue introducing him, Shakespeare takes great pains to emphasize his superiority to mere money (though he has immense quantities of it), the depth of his lore, his legendary reputation. But in the actual resuscitation of Thaisa, occult practices are altogether absent: the text mentions only warmth, coverings, music, and a vial of medicine

---

* Either of the "actresses" impersonating Thaisa and Marina could have doubled as Diana; the Lord God, on the other hand, who in Gower's poem directly instructed Apollonius, could not possibly be represented on stage.

from his store.* It is the Shakespearean language that swells
him beyond a mere practitioner to a vast shadowy figure
who speaks of attaining divine powers, even immortality,
through virtue and cunning. (A very powerful word that
last, in the Elizabethan theater; as in Jonson's *Alchemist*, the
cunning-man is specifically skilled in occult practices.)
Through long practice and painful study Cerimon has made
familiar

> To me and to my aid the blest infusions
> That dwells in vegetives, in metals, stones.†
>
> (III.ii.35–6)

Following in the footsteps of Egyptian physicians, who used
to be able to restore the dead to life, he surrounds the operation (which on the stage is the easiest of easy tricks) with
all the mysterious and arcane trappings of immemorial learning.‡ The exotic liquor in his vial would be the elixir, through
which alone he might aspire to immortality himself and
achieve renewed life for Thaisa; the signs, passes, and incantatory gestures with which any competent actor could be
trusted to enrich his performance of Cerimon would suggest
traditional magic formulas; and the background music, what-

---

* In III.ii.92, I read the "violl" of Q as "viall" (Q4)—(1) lest the boxes be
brought in to no purpose, (2) so the "resurrection" shall not seem easy
and commonplace, and (3) to accord with Gower, who says that Cerimon
"putte a liquour in hire mouth / Which is to few clerkes couth."

† Cerimon's "aid" is presumably his aide, or assistant, who in Gower's
telling of the story performs the actual restoration of Thaisa; in diminishing his role to that of a mere drudge, Shakespeare focusses attention
on Cerimon himself.

‡ In line 86 the substitution of Egyptian doctors for an Egyptian patient
involves resort to Wilkins' *Painful Adventures*, which not only refers to
Egyptian doctors but does so in crypto-blank-verse of very respectable
quality. The point of the allusion is to bring to mind Hermes Trismegistus,
founder of the entire hermetic tradition of occult knowledge.

ever its instrumentation, would be the Platonic, Pythagorean, or Orphic harmonies, such as were deemed to bring soul and body into intimate concord with one another.

Whether Cerimon was modelled on Paracelsus, Cornelius Agrippa, Giordano Bruno, John Dee, or some avant-garde but anonymous Rosicrucian is, of course, impossible to know. Shakespeare was not liberal in strewing unmistakable contemporary references through his writings, the locale of *Per.* is distant antiquity, not contemporary Europe, and in view of the play's remote and misty setting, the audience's imagination would better be turned toward the vague past than toward the controversial present. The two figures that Shakespeare would *not* want his audience to think of while looking at Cerimon would be Doctor Subtle and Captain Face—and they really were modelled on contemporary magicians.

So let Cerimon represent the ancient occult tradition, and his music the most remote and romantic music of which we know; the music of Orpheus would be particularly appropriate to the present circumstance of recalling a lost wife from the underworld. (And if Shakespeare could have known the music of Christof Willibald Gluck, who can doubt that he would have specified it for the resurrection-scene?)

But, looking at the text as for better or worse it is, no proper occasion really appears for hanging Orphic decorations on it. Cerimon is not, and does not want to be, Thaisa's husband; he has not braved the perils of the underworld to bring her back; his music is an adjunct to his art, not its essence; and the music he commands was so common a receipt for composing the spirits that Robert Burton wrote a full chapter on it (*Anatomy*, Part II, Sec. 2, Mem. 6, Subs. 3). As a matter of fact, the play sharply diminishes the musical accomplishments of Pericles as strongly emphasized by both Gower and Twine—in their versions he plays for a while the role of music master to Thaisa. The drama has none of this, though the passage in Gower is quite substantial, hence not at all easy to overlook. If Pericles is no musician in the play, that is no accident.

Not that Orpheus should, for these or any such reasons, be banished entirely from our reading of *Per.* III.ii; but his overtones must be muted and attenuated. The music itself, for which Cerimon calls perhaps twice, has to be heard by the audience; it is the one part of the enchantment process actually present to them. But Orpheus can be no more than a fading connotation—were he sensibly on stage or explicitly in the text, he would be as much out of place as Jonah or Lazarus. The myth of Orpheus is one strain of several that, even while remaining faintly perceptible individually, fold together to make of Cerimon's scene a resonant, isotonic chord.

A similar effect is achieved by different means in the other scene where music plays an active role in *Per.* It follows the moment of mutual recognition between Marina and her father in the harbor of Mytilene (V.i) when the hero, ecstatic with bliss at the recovery of his daughter, speaks almost incoherently, twice calling for fresh garments, and twice asking about certain music that he hears. The fresh garments are, dramatically, out of the question; Pericles cannot well disrobe on stage or retreat bashfully to the tiring room. But whether the audience should be given some actual music at this point is a long-standing critical crux. Though the play's text contains no stage-direction on the matter, it is such a scrappy piece of mixed-up typography, that one need have little compunction about emending it. But the dialogue itself seems to forbid:

> PER. —But what music?
> HEL. My lord, I hear none.
> PER. None?
> The music of the spheres! List, my Marina.

LYS. It is not good to cross him; give him way.
PER. Rarest sounds! Do ye not hear?
LYS. Music, my Lord? I hear.
PER.   Most heavenly music.
                                        (V.i.225 ff.)

The reactions of the three persons surrounding Pericles can be followed closely. Helicanus, old, loyal, and doggedly truthful, hears nothing, and says he hears nothing. When Pericles appeals to Marina, she is clearly embarrassed; her silence must mean that she cannot agree with her father and is reluctant to contradict him. Lysimachus rescues her; in saying "I hear," he confirms, though in the most minimal of ways,* the king's impression. Of all the characters on stage, Pericles is in a state of high, almost hysterical excitement; Marina, clearly, is not. She has been explaining her life history in a cool, factual way, and says not a single word of any sort at the discovery her father is not dead after all, but present before her. No wonder she, like the other dispassionate characters, hears no music.

Shakespeare, in fact, is in a bit of a hurry to wrap up his story. The effect of the music Pericles hears is almost comically abrupt; it puts him instantly to sleep. But of course it is not just a quiet nap; it is the sacred, visionary sleep in which Diana appears to tell him where his wife is. And for this sleep the music of the spheres or (if this is just hyperbole) some other heavenly harmonies are an indispensable preliminary.

---

* Lysimachus, in saying "I hear," speaks absolute truth; his auditory apparatus is unimpaired. In the circumstances, he is understood to say "I hear what you hear," which clearly he doesn't. Technically, this is tergiversation. Some editors have transferred the "I hear" speech to Pericles; but this doesn't strengthen or clarify the position of either character. Not for the first time in Shakespeare, the text here is subtler than the commentators.

So should the audience hear the music? Pericles hears it, but no other character on stage really does. There's no worming out of the contradiction, whichever actor gets to speak that indecisive "I hear." Pericles is the only one who hears anything. Yet, theatrically, it's too tantalizing to have music talked about on stage, to have it exercise tangible influence on a character, and not to present it somehow to the ears of the audience. There is no single decisive answer to the problem, but a contrivance-solution might be to have the audience, so far as possible, hear and not hear the music at the same time. That is, a musical phrase might be played faintly from a distance at a long interval of stage-time from Pericles' questions about it. To his first question, then, the audience-answer might be, "I think there was a little snatch of melody some time ago," and after this final affirmation they should wait, wait, wait till after a while the attentive ones are rewarded with a last mocking tail-end of disappearing phrase. (Perhaps it could be heard in the interval between one scene and the next, best when Pericles is asleep.) Shakespeare not infrequently wants to have it both ways, to suggest the contrary of what he represents, or to take away with a counter-reality something of what he has built up with his imaginings.

Where is Pentapolis? Well, for sure, it's where good king Simonides reigns—as any fisherman on the nearby seacoast could tell you. It's also where Pericles prince of Tyre went after fleeing from wicked King Antiochus; from Antioch he first went home to Tyre, and then, not yet feeling safe, continued on to Tarsus, where, with his fleet full of grain, he relieved the famine of the wretched inhabitants. Later, word reaching him at Tarsus of Antiochus' continued hostile intent, he took sail again and, having been shipwrecked, dragged himself to shore, dripping and solitary, near Pentapolis.

But, just a minute. Tyre lies along the coast of the eastern

Mediterranean, just about 200 miles south of Antioch; Tarsus is to the northeast of Antioch, less than a hundred miles away across the Gulf of Alexandretta. Pericles, in fleeing from the murderous assailants despatched against him by Antiochus, must, to reach Tarsus from Tyre, have sailed directly by his enemy's stronghold.* After leaving Tarsus Pericles proceeds, as noted, to Pentapolis, either of two kingdoms comprising five cities; and here is another awkward dilemma for the literal-minded. For one Pentapolis is on the coast of North Africa, where the best known of its five cities is Cyrene, and this is rather a far reach from Tarsus and Tyre. The other Pentapolis is in equal measure too close; it is the island of Lesbos, where there are five cities, the best known of which is Mytilene. On the one hand, Pentapolis as Lesbos creates inconceivable practical problems for the story. On the other hand, it would be strange if Pericles, ignoring the many refuges available to him on Crete, Cyprus, in Asia Minor, and the Aegean Sea, should sail across the open Mediterranean, only to find disastrous shipwreck off North African Pentapolis. Even stranger would be his course when, after marrying Thaisa, he starts off to return to Tyre, but encounters a storm off Ephesus, where Thaisa is "buried" at sea. From North Africa he is more than 700 miles out of his way, heading due north instead of east, and plunging once again across open ocean instead of prudently coasting along the Libyan, Egyptian, and Phoenician coastlines to Tyre. His wanderings from Tyre to Tarsus and back again, from one Pentapolis to another (if there really are two of them), have

* There cannot be much doubt that Tarsus is indicated by the word that Gower spells Tharse. The unusual Biblical form Tarshish can refer either to long-range ships in general, or to one of three destinations: Tartessus in Spain not far from Gades or Cadiz; Carthage in North Africa; or Ceylon off the coast of India. None of these fit well as the kingdom of Cleon and Dionyza. So, despite its awkward proximity to Antioch, let Tharse be Tarsus.

the quality of a long, anxious dream—like that from which
Odysseus, another sea-tossed wanderer, awoke when the
Phaeacians deposited him, fast asleep, on the coast of Ithaca.*
And in fact a normally unsuspicious viewer/reader of *Per.*
will take the Mediterranean peregrinations of Pericles very
much as a dream, within which Pentapolis is anywhere or
nowhere—at some convenient location or other, Greek in a
hazy sort of way, but perfectly receptive of a visiting prince
whose name may be Greek, but whose Tyrian origins are
probably semitic.

Persons no less than places have the translucent, discon-
nected quality of figures in a dream. Pericles has no parents
or relatives; he emerges as from a blank wall, a fully formed
prince of Tyre who without knowing her well, if at all, wants
to marry Antiochus' dangerous daughter. The name "Pericles" was bestowed on him, whether by Shakespeare or another, only when the legend of Apollonius (or Appollinus,
as Gower called him) was on the point of reaching the Globe's
wooden O. That he could no longer be Apollonius was determined by the conditions of English blank verse; but it is
unclear whether his new name made allusion to the Athenian

---

* Like Odysseus, Apollonius may have been, in early versions of the legend, a travelling merchant, one who sold grain instead of giving it to the
starving citizens of Tarsus. Reduplication is a constant feature of both
stories; wherever Odysseus sails, he finds avatars of Maya the weaver
dwelling in a cave and expecting him (Circe, Calypso, Arete, Penelope);
Pericles, wooing first in Antioch and then in Pentapolis, and twice shipwrecked into fortune, is twice bereaved and twice (most improbably)
reunited with his women. Like Mytilene (where they are celebrating the
feast of Neptune), Phaeacia (founded by descendants of Poseidon) is the
turning point of the wanderer's distresses; he must confront the perse-
cuting god in his own shrine. Like Odysseus, Pericles travels a long,
circuitous route to get back where he started from; like Pericles, Odysseus
must pass through a mean condition in order to assert, convincingly and
triumphantly, his royal character. Even in his unscissored locks and his
recurrent association with rebirth, Pericles displays the same residual
traces of an original sun-god that mark Homer's hero.

statesman or to Pyrocles, Prince of Macedon in Sidney's *Arcadia*. (That he has nothing to do with Spenser's Pyrochles, the embodiment of mindless rage, seems to be generally and mercifully agreed.) Neither of the possible originals of the name Pericles fits very well with the protagonist of the play; the statesman was not a traveller and the prince of Macedon was far from a model of patience. But Shakespeare, or whoever selected the name for the play, may have counted on the discords, and valued them, as in a title like "Lady Macbeth of Mtsensk."

In rearranging the names of the traditional story for dramatic presentation, the concerns of the dramatic workmen are generally pretty evident; the state of the case can be summarized in a table:

Play	Gower or Twine
Pericles	Apollinus (G); Apollonius (T)
Simonides	Artestrathes (G & T)
Cleon	Strangulio (G & T)
Lysimachus	Athenagoras
Helicanus	Hellican
Escanes	(no such person)
Thaliard	Taliartus
Cerimon	(Same name)
Leonine	Theophilus
Pandar	Leonine (G); master-bawd (T)
Boult	(unnamed servant)
Antiochus	(same name)
Philemon	(no such person) (G); Machaon (T)
Thaisa	P's wife (unnamed)
Marina	Thais (G); Tharsia (T)
Dionyza	Dionise (G); Dionisiades (T)
Philoten	(same name) (G); Philomacia (T)
Lychorida	(same name) (G); Ligozides (T)

Bawd   (no such person)
Nameless daughter of   (unnamed)
   Antiochus

Where names would be hard to remember, distinguish, or
pronounce, they were simplified; the inappropriate name of
a murderer (Theophilus) was changed to Leonine, which
used to be the name of the pandar (Latin *leno*, pimp); for
Athenagoras regent of Mytilene the name Lysimachus was
substituted—it may or may not be an accident that an historical Lysimachus was once military governor of the district
that includes Mytilene. It may or may not be significant that
Thais was the name of a famous Greek courtesan who accompanied Alexander the Great on his oriental conquests.
That Marina is called "Tharsia" in Twine's version and in
his original the *Gesta Romanorum* may, but does not necessarily, signify something about Pericles' intentions in settling
her (more or less permanently?) in Tarsus (Tharsus). Marina's
name is the most pointedly significant of those supplied for
the play; it is exceptional among the new names in being of
Latin rather than Greek origin; and it falls within the family
of names deriving more or less directly from "Mary." On
the title page, Quartos 1–3 printed her name as "Mariana"—
she is of course Marina in the text, where the origin of her
name is explained no fewer than four times. No doubt it
would be a very different play indeed if she were known as
"Thalassia."
   The bonding of Diana (the moon) and the sea is close and
traditional; interpreters who feel the play as it has come down
to us needs something more in the way of a unifying moral
have sought it in two passages, one early, the other late.
King Simonides, making excuses to his daughter's other suit-
ors, says something polite to them (II.v.11–12) about a vow
she has made to Diana; since nothing more is ever heard of
it, it passes (as it would in common society and in any play

less scrutinized than this) for a polite social lie. But if taken legalistically, and given such emphasis as the playwright wholly failed to provide for it, a vengeful and almost Calvinistic Diana might then be held responsible for the prolonged suffering of Pericles and his family. It is hard to know whether Pericles' perils at Antioch and first shipwreck at Pentapolis would then be regarded as promissory punishments for a crime he had yet to commit, or attributed to another deity entirely. One would have to work this out.

Less distinct but more ambitious is the second passage making for a moral structuring of the play; it implies nothing less than the transfiguring of Prince Pericles. In the blur of ecstatic impressions sweeping over him after the recognition scene with Marina, his mind tries to reach out and grasp the full wonder of what she has done and who she is; and he cries,

> O come hither,
> Thou that beget'st him that did thee beget,
> Thou that wast born at sea, buried at Tarsus,
> And found at sea again.
>
> (V.i.194 ff.)

The lines, especially the paradoxical second one (195), can be understood as paralleling the ancient Christian amphibole of Mary the creature of God giving birth in the Christ child to the God himself who was her begetter; thematically, this would tie in, as a violent contrast, to the wicked incest of Antiochus and his daughter. In the measure, then, that Pericles is deemed to be contaminated by his contact with incest in the first act, he can be supposed redeemed by this half-prophetic vision of the vicarious atonement.

No doubt the notion of human Mary giving birth, in baby Jesus, to the Third Person of the Trinity with all his perquisites and attributes was an old theme; Prudentius and

Venantius Fortunatus had been no strangers to it, and poets were still toying with it through the 17th century in sacred epigrams and devotional meditations. But in a dramatic speech, like Pericles', the formula comes with extra encumbrances. Suppose Marina to be Mary: Pericles must be either the begotten (infant Jesus) or the begetter (God the Father). However highly he values his newfound daughter, these must appear unseemly comparisons. Indeed, one might catch in passing at an analogy with the Trinity as line 195 of Act V, scene i slipped by; but if one were allowed a second thought, it would only be to reject its first implications as immoderate and grotesque. The persistence of the sea in Marina's life story is an authentic ground-bass; to borrow Pericles' potent word, one can hear it humming through the play. But parallels with the life of the Virgin are few, scanty, and likely to be strained. Marina's burial at Tarsus and rebirth from a brothel are jokes that waver on the edge of cruelty. As for the notion that Pericles was somehow rendered guilty of incest because he exposed it in others, no audience on earth could be expected to have that reaction—or if so, only by remote and indirect contamination from another legend.

For it is true that Pericles as he confronts the deadly riddle of Antiochus resembles Oedipus confronting the riddle of the sphinx; and it is true, to invoke Fluellen's famous argument, that there is incest in both. But the incest theme is actually the prime point of difference. Oedipus by answering the sphinx's riddle in a single word, opens the door to discovering what it is to be a man—what guilt one becomes liable to, what depths are revealed, by a desire to know the truth about oneself. Pericles learns nothing about himself; having fled from Antioch, he never again (so far as we are told) thinks spontaneously of the cruel king and his nameless daughter. Yet in one other basic aspect he does resemble Oedipus; for both of them, to answer the riddle is just as dangerous as to fail of answering it. They are victims of powers above, who made the circumstances around them, and made them unalterable. But there resemblance ceases. Under the bludgeonings of fate, Pericles is more pathetic than iron-souled Oedipus. He complains, acts erratically; except for the play-combats of the tournament, there is no single opponent to whom he stands up directly, including Fate or Destiny. His prevailing passivity is one reason why his sufferings seem, not only unmerited, but non-significant.

Pericles at the court of Antiochus would have been easy to portray as a rash or guilty or unscrupulous man; there is no sign of it. Thaisa amid the various festivities at Pentapolis might have been shown as violating any of several decorums, or as crossing somehow the easy temper of good king Simonides; a monitory oracle, a mysterious old codex, might have made the narrative's progress less routine. Pericles— who represents a stage in the degeneration of Odysseus down to Leopold Bloom—does not even take any active steps to get back his kingdom of Tyre until he receives letters from that city amounting practically to an ultimatum. So far as we can judge, the characters bring about neither the misfortunes with which for years they are overwhelmed nor the happy ending to which they are led. Shakespeare has not in fact shielded us carefully from thinking that their greatest troubles are of their own making. Pericles waits fourteen unnecessary years before trying to communicate with Marina at Tarsus, though he knows that's where she is, and the distance is negligible. Thaisa, recovered from the billows by Cerimon, never tries to communicate with (let alone, go to) Tyre and find out about Pericles; instead, she locks herself up impromptu in Diana's nunnery. Dionyza, finding that Marina casts her own daughter in the shade, never thinks of sending the unwelcome guest to Tyre or Pentapolis, but determines, without balancing the alternatives, to have her murdered. Neither Marina nor her faithful nurse Lychorida ever considers getting in touch with her royal kinfolk.

Even more startling are the undisguised peripeties of Fortune in the play. Cerimon's discovery of Thaisa in her waterproof coffin within hours of her being cast overboard can only be viewed with an indulgent smile; Marina's rescue from Leonine by the pirates is a *coup de théâtre* worthy of *The Perils of Pauline*; the accidental arrival of Pericles at Mytilene (whither, for unfathomable reasons, he has sailed from Tarsus, instead of going home to Tyre) stretches coincidence to the snapping point. In a manipulated world where things like this can happen, the bestowal of Marina on Lysimachus, managed offhandedly in a subordinate clause at the last minute, ought to come off as easily as any other bit of stage contrivance aimed at disposing of an unattached nubile ingenue before final curtain.

That it doesn't so come off is doubtless due in part to the shorthand quality of the last act. Since her triumph over the brothel environment and her recognition by Pericles, Marina is understood to be a pearl of great price, the very emblem of virgin purity; now she is handed over, without a word of her speaking, to a man whom the audience has seen only as a practiced whoremaster trying to buy a nice clean girl in a brothel. The play's handling of the matter is particularly unfortunate because it manages to encompass the worst of three alternatives. In the opening passages of the scene it makes unmistakably clear what Lysimachus is up to in the brothel—makes clear, too, that he has been a regular patron. Halfway through the scene, his character and the reasons for his presence change radically (after remarkably little urging from Marina). Now he says that *if* he had come there with evil intent, her words would have converted him. This is unconvincing, not only because she has said very little, but because his cheery opening remarks, inquiring the price of "a dozen of virginities" point the other way, and because no alternative reason for his being in such a place is ever provided.

Wilkins' novel is at least consistent. His Lysimachus is a hard-boiled whoremaster; he deals with the pimps, presses Marina to submit, and when she resists, "begins to be more rough with her." In an extended speech, she then rebukes him, as a result of which he confesses: "I hither came with thoughts intemperate, foul, and deformed, the which your pains have so well laved that they are now white." Then, in an episode transcribed from Twine, Lysimachus gives her gold, and pretends to leave the brothel. But he lingers in hiding to verify her continence, watches the next customer enter and leave, frustrated as he had been; and so, after conference with him, concludes that Marina is a genuinely good girl and must be protected.

Dramatically, Wilkins' is the better version, on several scores; it does not muddle Lysimachus' motivation, it gives Marina a speech which can at least pretend to be persuasive, it does not reduce her danger to a mere charade, and it heightens the anguish of her position. For what hope does she have when the highest of local authorities is hand in glove with the scoundrels and pimps who own her? On the other hand, making Lysimachus a serious threat to Marina's virginity in the whorehouse contaminates him almost irredeemably as a potential husband for this votaress of Diana.

But there was a third alternative. Gower's version of the story not only avoided all the inconveniences but provided a much more natural motivation for the action. By pleading with the brothel-keeper's man (Boult in the play) on the only level at which he can be reached, Marina persuades him (and through him the brothel-keeper) that she is worth more money for her polite accomplishments (teaching needle-craft, dancing, singing, unspecified intellectual skills) than as a common prostitute. Indeed, she is clever enough to point out that while she preaches virtue in his establishment, she is bad for business—blackmailing him, as it were, with a threat of moral propaganda. Thus she escapes from the stews; Athenagoras/Lysimachus never has to approach her there; she is respectably placed when he first meets her, and when she is shown to be a princess, their marriage is as good as made.

In asking why Shakespeare took clearly the worst of his alternatives in dealing with the brothel-scene, we have to ask why he made so much more of it than his predecessors had done. Counting lines, if only approximately, less than five percent of Gower's poem is devoted to the heroine's residence in the brothel, while more than fifteen percent of Shakespeare's lines deal with it. Moreover, at least half of Shakespeare's lines are devoted to broad talk among the bawds, pimps, and clients of the house. Their leering, witty, allusive exchanges create the atmosphere of sunken depravity through which Marina must move. It's not so much sexual license that makes the brothel as the callous buying and using of women till they are rotten with disease and must be discarded as so much filth. Shakespeare is careful not to introduce on stage any of the actual prostitutes; Doll Tearsheet, appearing in the house at Mytilene, might be either defiant or pathetic, but in either case she could only diminish the hatefulness of the management—she would be a fellow-victim, not a monster.

Shakespeare wanted the whorehouse scenes in his drama, as he wanted the scene with the three fishermen near Pentapolis and the two storms at sea because they provided strong scenes and memorable lines within an otherwise talky and slow-paced charade. They are the verbal meat of the drama. Briefly, he seems to have been more interested in the scene than in the participants, in the language than in the characters. As long ago as *Henry IV, Part I*, he was ready to lay aside the telling of a straight story to eavesdrop on the gutter-talk of a set of common carriers. Here the business-talk of the keepers, their immersion in the squalor of their trade, is emphasized by the hypocrisies they must put on

when dealing with a "gentleman" like Lysimachus. "O, sir,
I can be modest," says Boult—no doubt with a smirk; and
Lysimachus enthusiastically agrees: pimps must talk nice and
whores pretend to be chaste. They both know how things
are done; indeed they fit together, hand in glove. At the
bottom of society, as at the bottom of human nature where
we are all animals together, it's a dirty business that won't
stand too much talking about. Marina, who tries to rise above
it, perhaps to the sphere of Diana herself, occasionally comes
close to sounding like a Salvation Army lassie; no doubt that
is why Shakespeare displaced her lecture away from Lysimachus, transferring it to Boult.* He, as it happens, has an
answer for her, reminiscent of Mrs. Warren's reply to her
daughter in Shaw's play: essentially it is, "shame on you for
a stuck-up prude—how can you lecture me when you don't
know what it is to be the dirt and draff of society?" That
moment of truth Shakespeare saved for the end of his fourth
act; it doesn't curtail, but deepens the impact of the brothel-
scene in general—to which the character of Lysimachus is
frankly sacrificed. He is not allowed to stand safely aside
while Marina fights free; neither is he forced to recognize
the depth of his own involvement in the sexual underworld.
Boult, who is used to scapegoating for the gentry, takes the
brunt of the rhetoric and most of the opprobrium; and the
story, which had long ago decided to dispose of Marina to
someone of the eligible class, is in a way to being fulfilled.
After sounding the depths, the play is eager to return to the

---

* An eloquent rebuke of Lysimachus may have dropped out of the text of
Q; with printers like Gosson *et al.*, anything is possible. But Marina cannot
be giving her chastity-speech over and over; and anything tending to
equate Lysimachus with Boult would render his marriage with Marina
grotesque. The forced marriage of Mariana with Angelo at the end of
Measure for Measure has been cited as a precedent; but the circumstances
are utterly different.

surface, and so it does, with the most expendable character only slightly smeared, only a little dislocated.

Immersion in the foul waters of sexual servitude, as in the silent depths of the sea, is itself (rather than the resurrection it foreshadows) the deepest scene of the play. Like Thaisa, Marina is recovered to a pallid, not to say questionable, domestic bliss of which she is never allowed an instant to express acceptance, let alone appreciation.

The depths touched by the play are deeper because of the tenuity of the central characters. Both ladies have attracted lyrical comment for their purity and innocence, but that is not to say much more than for their silence and vacancy; they are benign presences, hardly characters at all. Over the last three acts Thaisa has barely 25 lines to speak, while Marina says nothing at all to her newly recovered father and just ten words to her restored mother. Apart from characterization, the texture of the play is also thin because of the gaps between episodes and because old Gower, intruding repeatedly on the action, calls attention to the fact that it is a story, an old story, and a story many times told. Ostensibly, he intervenes to forward the plot and to invite the audience to exercise its imagination, but as a figure from an exotic time-frame (neither the "now" of the audience nor the "then" of the play), speaking a quaint dialect, and wearing, according to the title-page of Wilkins' novel, an unfamiliar costume, he intrudes on the action far more than he forwards it. The decision to bring him on stage, not just to speak prologue and epilogue, not just to introduce each new act, but to narrate within the last two acts as well—and several times to call specific attention to the artifice of the drama— will bear a good deal of reflection. Certainly the artist who hefted easily the stupendous actions of *Lear* and *Antony* without the aid of a chorus did not need one to tell this antique tale of domestic distresses and reconciliations. *The Two Noble*

Kinsmen, another collaborative play on an ancient text, pays explicit and generous tribute to Chaucer in its prologue, but dispenses with his services for the rest of the play, including the epilogue. The figure of old Gower in *Per.* must serve a dramatic end not altogether familiar in Shakespeare; perhaps it could be defined, in a preliminary way, as the distancing of the story in time. The more remote the story could be made to feel, the less its improbabilities would be felt to obtrude from the mists of antiquity. Its diffuse action and pallid characters called for it to be told in a series of spectacles or tableaux, the connections between which might sometimes want to be reinforced, sometimes overlooked. Gower's presence deprecated the story while at the same time authenticating it: "This is not our story, it's an old one (so don't expect it to make sense in modern terms); but at the same time it's genuine, it has the patina of age on it." Somewhere in the social background, the figure of Gower in *Per.* must have drawn on a renewed popular concern for the mythic English past such as grew up during early Stuart times in the wake of antiquarians like William Camden, John Selden, John Stow, Michael Drayton *et al.*; the historical parts of Shakespeare's next play, *Cym.*, seem to be tuned to the same frequency. Thus the figure of Gower, even in undermining the narrative, reinforces it.

A root fact that can't be overlooked in discussion of *Per.* is the fact that, however little it resembles a well-made play, the drama was popular in its time (witness all those Quartos) and can still be effective onstage today. Its constructional oddities can be overlooked or bypassed, its character-outlines filled from the reservoirs of an audience's natural human kindness. Cerimon's stage-sleights, as enriched by Shakespeare's verbal magic, can still be impressive; the concept of despondent old age roused to new life by youth, innocence, and love can still appeal to audiences. Not far behind most of the stage-personages, latent ethical abstractions—precisely

Youth, Innocence, Love, and their many associates—do make themselves felt, with effects that the individual can only calculate for himself. With the prefixed story of Antiochus and his daughter not much can be done, and the villainy of Dionyza and Cleon seems almost irresistibly schematic; but the brothel at Mytilene is an authentically louche place. The play vibrates imaginatively between the menacing and the holy, between despair and ecstasy; even if we don't feel the personages deeply, their adventures have color and suspense. The play has little motion and less depth but it vibrates with the idea of renewal.

REFERENCES

Philip Edwards, "An Approach to the Problem of Pericles" in *Shakespeare Survey* 5 (1952), argues that two different reporters were responsible for the manifest corruption of the text and for the sensible differences between the first two acts and the last three.

Sina Spiker, "George Wilkins and the Authorship of Pericles," in *Studies in Philology* XXX (1933), carefully examines the novel and the play, concluding that Wilkins copied the play as produced (with many additions from Twine), but was not himself one of the original authors.

C. L. Barber, "Thou that beget'st him that did thee beget" in *Shakespeare Survey* 22 (1969), seeks to describe and explain "the transformation of persons into virtually sacred figures who yet remain persons." The application is to *Per.* and *WT*; and the topic is one which only an acute mind would have defined. But, as between offering a literary explanation of Shakespeare's nuanced stage effects and attempting to psychoanalyze his stage characters, it's possible that Barber made the wrong choice.

III

CYMBELINE

To a much greater extent than *Per.* the play which goes (quite unfairly) by the name of one of its minor characters, Cymbeline, was clearly a conscious piece of stage carpentry. Such as it is, the fable of *Per.* came to Shakespeare's hands as a preformed unit. Some part of it may have already been cast in dramatic form; the entire plot was before him as he wrote, and he neither added nor subtracted very much—unless the presenter "Gower" is his addition. To align as well as to offset the two plays, it may be well to summarize here some of the major points both of difference and of similarity. Both *Per.* and *Cym.* deal with a distant, semi-Christian period of time, a divided but ultimately reunited family, a protagonist oppressed by fortune but restored with the help of coincidence, a central concern with chastity, an apparent resurrection from the dead, a sort of divine intervention at the end. *Per.* has a kind of heraldic villain, who makes a flourish in the first act and is hardly heard from again; *Cym.* has a pair of villains who remain present and active till fairly late in the play. *Cym.*'s protagonist is less exclusively passive than *Per.*'s; the play possesses, in addition, a jealousy-theme and a court-country, Italian-English, or cosmopolitan-provincial contrast. Unlike *Per., Cym.* does not have a presenter or chorus, does not have an authentic magician, and has no particular concern with the sea, its depths or its tempests. The action of *Per.* can cover little less than 16 or 17 years; that of *Cym.* (though everything is very indefinite) could be compressed within as little as one. *Per.* takes place in some dozen locales around the eastern Mediterranean; *Cym.* is much more localized.

This list of likes and unlikes could be extended, but already its character suggests the looseness of the ties that bind, as plays of a single "sort," the two romances. The extremely heterogeneous source materials entering into the plot of *Cym.*—they come from many different ages and regions of the world, from many different classes of books—also constitute a notable background fact.

1. The reigns of Cunobelin or Cymbeline and Guiderius (dating back roughly to the beginnings of the Christian era) were briefly and confusedly described by Holinshed, the 16th-century chronicler from whom Shakespeare had already gleaned material for his history plays. Here he would have found the story of the Romans' successful efforts to regain the tribute money extorted by Julius Caesar but allowed to lapse by his successor.

2. The tale of Posthumus' wager with Iachimo on the chastity of Imogen, Shakespeare found crisply narrated as story 9 of Day II in the *Decameron*; there the characters are named Bernabó Lomellin (of Genoa) and Ambrogiuolo (of Piacenza). Shakespeare may or may not have read Italian easily, but he could have read Boccaccio in a French translation, like that of Antoine Le Maçon. One way or another, he certainly knew the Boccaccio tale because he uses (in *Cym.* and in *WT* as well) some

of its most striking details. But he used a collateral source too. A very clumsy prose narrative titled *Frederyke of Jennen* (Genoa) had been printed in 1518 at Antwerp and reprinted (1520, 1560) in England; it is another version of the Boccaccio-tale (or of the narrative from which Boccaccio took his version), and it too has some distinctive details, which Shakespeare followed. The only conclusion is that they are joint sources.

3. The story of Imogen's love for Posthumus, aversion for Cloten, and flight to the cave of a banished and disgraced courtier (who is *not*, however, guarding the king's two missing sons but is instead Posthumus' long-lost father!) parallels and could have come from *The Rare Triumphs of Love and Fortune*, a play dating from the 1580's and published in 1589. The work is anonymous, primitive in its writing, and can be no more than a tertiary source behind Boccaccio, a certain, and *Frederyke of Jennen*, a very probable source. Major components of the Shakespeare narration are missing from the earlier play.

4. A second work by Holinshed, *The Historie of Scotland* (mostly translated from the Latin of Hector Boece), includes an account of the battle of Luncarty which closely parallels the heroic actions of Belarius, Guiderius, and Arviragus in their battle against the Romans.

5. In the story of Belarius and the stolen princes some analogies have been recognized with story 8 of Day II in the *Decameron*, i.e., that directly preceding the wager-story. But the analogies are not very close, and most opinion credits this bit of the play to common romance traditions and to Shakespeare's not-completely-negligible powers of literary invention.

6. In addition to Holinshed, the story of Cymbeline's reign could have reached Shakespeare in part through the *History* by Geoffrey of Monmouth; but this source would

contribute nothing distinctive, and there is no reason why Shakespeare should have gone back to Geoffrey's Latin when he had Holinshed's English close to hand.

7. For the names of characters, Shakespeare went hither and yon. Imogen or Innogen is named in Holinshed as the wife of Brutus, first ruler of Britain; she may also be found in *Faerie Queene* II.x.13. Cloten, Mulmucius, Sicilius, Cassibelan, Tenantius, Guiderius, and Arviragus are also to be found in Holinshed, and in one capacity or other, in one form or other, in *Faerie Queene* II.x as well. The name and birth of Posthumus Leonatus probably derive from a son born to Lavinia after the death of her husband Aeneas; the legend founded itself on *Aeneid* VI.763, to which the commentators added generously.

8. There is some likeness between the wicked queen (Imogen's step-mother) and an equivalent figure in the fairy-tale of Snow White; but the queen is akin to all the witches and sorceresses of legend, and the story about wicked stepmothers was so old and widespread that the character herself refers to it.

While considerable, the range of reading represented here is not out of the way for Shakespeare, but it pretty surely does not represent a deliberate search for mosaic-bits out of which to assemble a play. Shakespeare may have been asked by his company to scout through old materials in search of new play-stuff; he may have remembered, or have made notes on, bits and pieces of dramatic material from his random reading of the past. His apparent decisions to write after 1607 or so plays with less than monumental protagonists displaying less than labyrinthine inner lives may have entailed a good deal of literary rummaging and even more rearranging. The effects are clearly apparent in *Cym.*, a drama whose illogical juxtapositions, narrative improbabilities, and structural gaps put Doctor Johnson quite out of patience. Four or five distinct stories had to be integrated with one another; if they did not come together reluctantly, they occasionally had to be held together by main force. Cornelius explains in Act I that the medicine he is giving the queen isn't really a poison, then has to explain again in Act V that it wasn't; Belarius explains in Act III the story of the young princes that the audience already knew in Act I and will hear again in Act V. An unusually obvious scene-setting dialogue between two anonymous gentlemen, explanatory soliloquies of unusual directness, a mysterious but convenient "feigned letter," and some unashamed coincidences all build toward a busy last act in which everyone stands around explaining who he really is, why he's sorry for what he did, or why he isn't dead after all. It's almost as if Shakespeare's search for materials had been too successful for its own good; so many complications accumulate that by the end of the play only strenuous efforts by a contortion artist can get us out of them. The cramped conclusion is particularly obtrusive in view of the play's vacant mid-section, during which Posthumus—the "hero" of the play, such as he is—disappears from view for two full acts, and Cymbeline is lost from sight for almost three. Belarius and the two princes do not even set foot on stage till the middle of the third act.

The impression one gets from *Cym.* that in some ways the play is too full and in other ways too empty is a good place to start talking about it; Cymbeline himself and his close family provide a major center of vacancy. Hardly anyone has been able to overlook the fact that, as a king, Cymbeline is next thing to a nonentity. Indeed, his banishing of Posthumus sets the plot in motion; but he acts, we are given to understand, only at his queen's instigation, as a machine moved only by her crafty, greedy mind. In the conference with Lucius (III.i), he allows Cloten (of all people!) and the queen to usurp his position as royal spokesman; faced with the problems of a war he has too rashly invited, he finds himself at a loss how to carry it on (IV.iii). Having defeated the Romans through no merit of his own, he submits to imperial authority for no particular reason, and promises renewed tribute. In the process he lays blame for his original decision, rather meanly, on his wicked queen, now dead. Either defiance or compliance could have been made perfectly acceptable as a dramatic attitude; but to have a king shift from one to the other for no apparent reason, especially when men have given their lives on his first say-so, is intolerable. Both Posthumus and Iachimo, identifying a Roman war against England with a war against Imogen, shift allegiance indirectly or whole-heartedly from Rome to Britain. Yet the British king who first declared the war and in whose name it is ostensibly being fought, surrenders the principal issue the minute it is won, while nobody so much as says Boo to him.

Well, Cymbeline was never a character to inspire much liking. A monarch who could carelessly lose a couple of his own sons, whose wife manages him not only with ease but with contempt, who turns off and on his affection for Imogen with a twist of the tongue, and who is blind to merits in Posthumus, defects in Cloten, that everyone else sees, can hardly engage our sympathy. Kingship might be another matter. Because royal blood runs in their veins, Guiderius and Arviragus are repeatedly described as having noble instincts and heroic tempers. That their father is no such creature is bound to be observed, though the fact is nowhere explained. The same blood that made them lordly raptors seems to have made their father something of a chicken.

Posthumus Leonatus is the hero of the play, or at least the husband of its heroine; from the moment the curtain rises, he is proclaimed as the most accomplished and distinguished of men. But the things he says and does on stage fall well below the level of his press-notices. After submitting without protest to banishment, he brags indiscreetly at Rome about Imogen's virtue (this habit, we note, has got him in trouble before), and enters into a bet, humiliating under the best of circumstances to his wife's honor. To help scoundrelly Iachimo win the wager against her virtue, he writes a letter of flattering introduction, but accompanies it with not a word descriptive of his own concerns, activities, and feelings. Upon Iachimo's return, he accepts as proof of his wife's promiscuity weak circumstantial evidence, makes no effort to verify the story he has heard (for example, by consulting Pisanio), but breaks into a diffuse rant against women in general—a rant which verges at its conclusion on the ridiculous. Then he orders Pisanio to kill Imogen out of hand, without so much as considering the light in which this piece of base duplicity casts him.

Most of these contrived proceedings were given to Shakespeare by his antecedent sources; but when he transferred the wager-story a couple of stages up the social ladder, special difficulties accrued to it. Like Bernabó of Genoa, Ambrose of Jennen was of the merchant class—not by any means like Posthumus a courtier-soldier married to a princess. At the level of travelling salesmen, the vulgar jokes about fidelity come naturally into play; they are part of the thoroughly murky water in which the characters of *fabliaux* and *novelle* customarily swim. But Posthumus is supposed to be a gentleman, a man of honor, of unusual honor; the vulgar thought-processes and revenge schemes of suburban jealousy (getting, forsooth, the servants to take part in one's matrimonial quarrels!) seem to tarnish Posthumus the more because he has been burnished to such a high gloss by the testimony of those who know him. The adulation of Imogen, which is profuse and vocal, adds to the audience's sense of a disparity between Posthumus as he behaves and as he is described. She is forgiving beyond nature when she says not a word of reproach to her husband after learning that he has tried to have her murdered on no evidence more compelling than a mole on her breast. He has behaved atrociously; and the only way to keep the fact from being made apparent to the audience is to have her say nothing about it.*

Perhaps because the 19th century projected into Imogen its own cherished ideals of womanly character, she attracted for many years a good deal of lyrical commentary; contributing to this adulation was, undoubtedly, the fact that her part in the play is basically passive and pathetic. Especially in the early acts, she is a girl rather given to ecstasies and flights of strained fancy; for example, her anxieties over the details of Pisanio's farewells to Posthumus, and her excited impatience to get to Milford Haven, where she expects Posthumus will be. Though repeatedly described as a person of rare temper and quality (the gods themselves say so), she is not in fact possessed of much discernment. She fails utterly to see through Iachimo, fails to suspect the medications that Pisanio gives her as from the queen, and thinks, when she mistakes the headless body of Cloten for that of Posthumus, that Cloten and Pisanio have conspired to commit the murder—though she has no reason to suppose that Cloten is anywhere in the vicinity. To adopt momentarily the commercial idiom conspicuous in the play itself, she is handed a good deal of moral capital at the very start of the action, in that she has defied her pig-headed father and witch-stepmother in order to marry a man of high merit and humble though honorable stock. In the artificial world of the theater (provided only she is young, pretty, and appealing), that history is enough to align the sympathies of the audience solidly behind her. Yet for the rest of the play, it cannot be

---

* Of course the ease with which Pisanio induces Imogen to run off to Milford Haven only highlights the oddity of Posthumus' not being there to greet her in person, for execution or explanation. To put off on Pisanio a murder which, if it's to be done at all, he should perform himself, is the depth of ignominy.

said that she ever again contemplates a step of equivalent moral energy.

In fact both Imogen and her husband talk for a good part of their time a dialect pitched a good bit higher and more artificial than that of normal folk. Posthumus' diatribe against the female sex, after hearing the report of Iachimo, has already been noted as coming close to scaling the heights of absurdity; his threat to sit down and write a satire on women provokes amusing images, as of his failure to get the rhymes right and the meter smooth. As for Imogen, the extended departure speech she says she did not have time to deliver, and therefore does deliver to Pisanio and the audience, strains both language and her own dignity:

> I did not take my leave of him, but had
> Most pretty things to say: ere I could tell him
> How I would think on him at certain hours,
> Such thoughts and such: or I could make him swear
> The shes of Italy should not betray
> Mine interest and his honour; or have charg'd him
> At the sixth hour of morn, at noon, at midnight,
> T'encounter me with orisons, for then
> I am in heaven for him; or ere I could
> Give him that parting kiss, which I had set
> Betwixt two charming words, comes in my father,
>
> etc.
>
> (I.iv.25 ff.)

More even than the artifice of these girlish fancies, the self-consciousness of Imogen's speech strikes one. She deplores the missed opportunity to say pretty things, and though the charming words surrounding her last kiss may be supposed protections ("charms") against the world's perils, they can express just as well Imogen's satisfaction with her own imagined performance. Modern styles for the comportment of heroines will not approve such self-gratulation, but the mannerism fits with a certain verbal theatricality in the emotional life of the drama's "polite" characters.

Partly this was a condition of the story. The plot of the wager, as it shaped itself under the dramatist's hands, required that the lovers be physically separated from one another from Act I, scene ii to Act V, scene v. When they do occupy the same stage, they must share it, both at the beginning of the play and at the end, with numerous other characters. To create the impression that they care intensely for one another, they can only make highflown speeches. This is very much in the romance tradition where the sentimental foibles of the quality are pursued through the rough and tumble of the world's business, and distinguished from that business by verbal artifice. But it is also part of a major dramatic point after which Shakespeare seems to have been deliberately reaching, in *Cym.* as in the other romances, that is, a contrast between the florid and often dishonest wit of the court and the flat, even foolish, but genuine speech of the country.

Most apparent in the way of a skilfully contrived and manipulated dialect of falsity are Iachimo's speeches to Imogen. Like the virtuoso performance of Gloucester in wooing Lady Anne at the funeral of her murdered husband, Iachimo manages successively to slander Posthumus, to venture a direct pass at Imogen, and then to recover from his rebuff with unctuous flattery of the lady and particularly of her husband. Deftly blending incoherent hyperbole, sly insinuations, direct effrontery, and specious explanations, he overwhelms unworldly Imogen, whose previous practice in erotic maneuvering had been limited to rebuffing oafish advances by Cloten. Like his distant counterpart Iago, Iachimo is an artist of innuendo. Indeed, it is only by his simple little trick with the trunk that he gets the evidence to convince Posthumus; from a severely practical point of view, his efforts to deceive

and then seduce Imogen are not only useless but dangerous—at first sight of her, he realizes that his standard tricks
and devices are not going to do any good. But he goes ahead
with them anyway, so the audience can appreciate the link
between inveterate malice and rhetorical artifice—even, one
might say, role-playing. Iachimo is perhaps the most visible
of the many arch-actors who haunt Shakespeare's imagination because his rhetoric is most clearly an engine in the
hands of his greed, his arrogance, his cruelty—in short, his
"Italian" nature.

Another skirmish between court and country language occurs when Arviragus the younger prince, lamenting the supposed death of Fidele, speaks words of neo-Arcadian elegy
to the corpse. They are quite beautiful words in themselves,
and in the 18th century William Collins, ignoring the actual
dirge sung by the two princes nearby, wove Arviragus'
speech into a second "Dirge in Cymbeline," which is itself
one of the jewels of the language. But the older brother,
Guiderius, will have none of it:

> Prithee have done,
> And do not play in wench-like words with that
> Which is so serious.
>
> (IV.ii.229 ff.)

It is a curious rebuke, for the two brothers are, otherwise,
almost always at one in their sentiments. In the dramatic
context, they are severe young men, brought up in rugged
surroundings by a strict father, hunters and warriors on instinct. They are English, therefore (according to the mythology) possessed of the "natural" virtues, uncontaminated
by the languors and luxuries of the decadent Mediterranean
countries. Yet they are also poets on instinct, and the dirge
they sing or pronounce antiphonally over the dead Fidele
will provide one of the most impressive moments of the

drama. All these tempered elements may be supposed to combine with their instinctive royal nobility to attune their attitude toward fine language. But the contrast with the pretty words that Imogen regrets she did not get to speak could hardly be sharper.

The opposition between blunt-but-honest and intricate-but-deceptive language is not always made directly and does not always point at the same judgment. The queen's son Cloten is, in the Elizabethan idiom, a "natural," and in stage idiom a "heavy," but in both capacities so inept as to provide a major source of entertainment in the play. Lest the audience miss the point of his foolishness, Shakespeare has provided for his appearances in I.iii and II.i a Second Lord whose only function is to comment sarcastically on Cloten's deficiencies of wit and courage. Strictly, this is unnecessary; Cloten is amply capable of scoring points against himself; indeed, he is notably careless about his own defence. His manners are atrocious, his speech is uncouth, and his persistence in the face of Imogen's open antipathy uncivilized. Yet, as in Caliban (and King Ubu as well), there is a strain of grotesque poetry in Cloten, not unrelated to his natural condition. He is utterly without restraint over his appetites or shame about indulging them; it pleases him to think he can "commit offence to his inferiors," sulk when he loses at games, and bluster when he wins. On matters of his own dignity, he is very touchy, though he has to be instructed what they are; and he has just wit enough to realize that Imogen is pretty, though by no means enough to devise a way for earning her liking. He is appetite inchoate and undirected. He wants to fight everyone, kill Posthumus, imitate Posthumus by wearing his clothes, rape Imogen, disgrace Imogen, be loved by Imogen—a chaos of contradictory, infantile impulses. Even his depravity is almost charming in its openness; recruiting Pisanio for his service, he promises that if "I should have cause to use thee with a serious industry, that is, what villainy soe'er I bid thee do, to perform it directly and truly, I would think thee an honest man." Or again, standing outside Imogen's casement, he says, with a kind of round-eyed bemused innocence worthy of Bottom the Weaver, "I am glad I was up so late, for that's the reason I was up so early."

Such is Cloten, half monster, half simpleton—blustering, gross, and incapable of carrying out a fraction of the mischief boiling at the bottom of his psyche. In all these attributes he resembles Bremo, the wild man of that old chestnut, *Mucedorus*, and not least in the ease with which, after he has glowered and domineered around the stage, he is dispatched by the first opponent who lifts a hand to put him down. "Paper tiger" is too kind an expression for Cloten, but it points the right way. Why then are this grotesque fellow and his witch-mother allowed the strongest lines in the interviews with Lucius (III.i and v) which, by rejecting Roman demands for tribute, determine the war to follow? The praise of England as a little world in itself (even if it didn't reverberate in the ears of its hearers against famous patriotic speeches like that of Gaunt in Act II of *Richard II*) must surely have roused the enthusiasm of the groundlings; Cloten's rude wit about Roman noses would stand out vividly against the polite, neutral formulas of diplomacy. Though otherwise despicable or ludicrous, Cloten attracts in these scenes strong impulses of national pride—all the stronger, no doubt, because of an implicit parallel with recent protestant rejection of demands from Rome for ecclesiastical tribute. Even more important surely than what Cloten says in rejecting Roman demands is the way he says it, with comic exaggeration and rough, country humor, with no deference at all.

In this context, an acute and original suggestion of Homer D. Swander (see the reading list at the end of this chapter) that Posthumus and Cloten are linked by more intimate bonds than those of mere rivalry seems particularly *à propos*. They resemble one another physically to the point of being able to wear one another's clothing. Posthumus must be purged of some of Cloten's grossness, and Cloten before he dies acquire some of Posthumus' belligerent bravery and then the likeness will not be at all strained. As they never occupy the same stage together, they might well be played by the same actor. And to the extent that Cloten foreshadows Caliban, his ambiguous intimacy with Posthumus touches a chord that will be sounded again in the love-hate grapple of Caliban and Prospero.

Strikingly, though Cloten elsewhere in the play is an empty braggart, that is not his role in the conference with Lucius. Cymbeline (who has evidently conned his Holinshed recently) points out that the Pannonians and Dalmatians are already in revolt against imperial exactions (III.i.74). It is a precedent that the Britains without "coldness," i.e., cowardice, cannot decline; and in the final interview with Lucius, Cymbeline adds an even more strong and direct argument against the demands of the emperor:

> Our subjects, sir,
> Will not endure his yoke; and for ourself
> To show less sovereignty than they, must needs
> Appear unkinglike.
>
> (III.v.4 ff.)

That "sovereignty" of the freeborn Englishman is shown onstage by Cloten; allowing him to voice it identifies him for the moment with the national spirit—until, even before scene v of Act III is concluded, he resumes his bestial character in a couple of incoherent, furious tirades against Imogen and Posthumus. If he represents in some measure the national spirit, Shakespeare is evidently of two minds about that spirit. He makes the point even stronger in a clearly managed scene (V.iii) between Posthumus (exhausted from the heat of battle) and a finical British Lord who, having run away, now stops to ask "What news?" Like Hotspur in a similar situation, Posthumus answers with bitter contempt, offering him a pitiful versicle ("wench-like words" or "holiday and lady terms") with which to prettify the grim facts of battle, and in the end driving the shamefaced Briton away. Here, evidently, is another and even more contemptible incarnation of the national spirit.

Shakespeare, in contriving the play, had several uses for the scene with the British Lord. It provided occasion for Posthumus to describe the heroic stand of Belarius and the princes, while at the same time demonstrating heroic reticence by suppressing his own part in the battle. But nothing in the dramatic situation requires that the British Lord be an abject coward, except that such a character undercuts Cloten's recent boast (III.v.20) that "your valiant Britons have their wishes in it," i.e., the war. It was Caesar's judgment, which Posthumus endorses by quoting it (II.iv), that the Britons, though undisciplined, were brave; in Cloten we see that they are thoroughly undisciplined, and in the British Lord that their valor leaves a good deal to be desired. Perhaps Shakespeare was simply preparing his audience for the compromise solution to the war, in which Cymbeline suddenly surrenders the *casus belli* in the very moment of his victory. Perhaps also he was taken with a contrast between court- and country-warriors, between gallants and mountaineers, carpet-knights and sinewy infantry-men. The original of Belarius in Holinshed's chronicle of Scotland was not a banished courtier, but a plowman, a peasant named Haie; his gallant helpers were not a pair of lost princes, but his sons.*

---

* And when one looks at it from this angle, isn't the story of the lost princes patched into the play rather more clumsily than is usual for Shakespeare?—first in the introductory conversation of the two gentlemen, who themselves find the story they recite incredible; and then in the notion that the princes' bold, audacious character is due to their descent from the bland and colorless Cymbeline?

Actually, it isn't one, but a set of contrasts that are inter-twined here. The rudeness of a cold cave in Wales plays against the luxury represented in Imogen's bedroom. The nerve and muscle of lonely mountain hunters play against the society clustering around the king—not just Cloten, but the jeering courtiers who make fun of Cloten. The passionate veracity of Posthumus—even when he acts like a fool—plays against the cheap cynicism, and equally cheap repentance, of Iachimo. The witch queen who sophisticates flowers into poison plays against the flowers laid on Fidele's tomb; the hired musicians of Cloten against the plainsong of the griev-ing princes; the instinctive affection of the boys for their sister against the peremptory authority of Cymbeline's court; and the hearty, macabre jocosity of Posthumus' jailer in the last act against Iachimo's longwinded lachrymose whining. Be-hind all these oppositions, and partly combined with them, is a contrast between the provincial integrity of Britain and the cosmopolitan corruption of Rome—or is it to be called Italy?

The play itself offers a curious contrast in usages here, for in fact Lucius and the various Roman officials who take part in the play are necessarily Italians just as much as Iachimo is. But Rome is the term for political and military power, and along these lines Roman manliness is much emphasized. When Cymbeline says that all the Roman captives must be executed (but an audience must presume he doesn't mean, or doesn't know, what he's saying, for the threat is left floating in the air), Lucius takes the menace stoically: "A Roman with a Roman's heart can suffer" (V.v.81). Toward the very end of the play, the Roman soothsayer delivers himself of a vision in which the imperial eagle somehow (not very distinctly) mingles his favor with the radiant Cymbeline, so that as part of the empire England is exalted. And the presence of that image at the end cannot help reminding us of the eagle-imagery that has persistently clung to Posthumus

(I.ii.70; I.v.11; etc.). He is, after all, a Roman with a Roman name, though also ambiguously a Briton; the one thing he is not in any way is an Italian, and that because he is an eagle, a noble or even a royal emblem, and Italians are almost always in this play bad. In Act V this vituperation of things Italian comes to a double climax with the contrite Iachimo's laying the blame for his behavior on "mine Italian brain," and Posthumus' fierce outburst a few lines later, "Italian fiend!" (V.v.196, 210). But in the background lie phrases like "this yellow Iachimo," "what false Italian," and "drug-damn'd Italy" (II.iv; III.ii; III.iv). For any such concentrated, reiterated mass of invective there is no precedent in the sources—nor, indeed, in previous plays of Shakespeare. Mario Praz, in a well-known essay on "Shakespeare's Italy," rightly emphasizes that Shakespeare rarely gives us the "black" Italian who so delighted the lurid imagination of Webster and Ford—that prowling, treacherous villain armed with poison ring, stiletto, and a copy of Machiavelli. But Praz wholly overlooks this play of *Cym.*, as well as an earlier and lesser example of its contrast between Italian corruption and English integrity. The occasion for Gaunt's famous burst of deathbed eloquence on the glories of Britain (*Richard II*, II.i) was York's remark that Richard had been seduced by

> Report of fashions in proud Italy,
> Whose manners still our tardy apish nation
> Limps after in base imitation.

Since the days of Roger Ascham, if not earlier, this complaint about English subservience to Italian immorality had been stock; Shakespeare had, by and large, abstained from it, but here, with hateful Iachimo to contrast with Posthumus the angel of light, he lets out all the stops. Indeed, the contrast would be pretty flat and mechanical if the idea of Rome did not intervene, casting a bit of imperial luster over the otherwise sparsely realized accommodation of Cymbeline with his courtly antagonist and his defeated legions.

Another way in which Shakespeare prevented the play from working itself out too flatly was, we may surmise, by adding two exalted and distracting pieces of stage business to the already crowded fifth act. Posthumus, falling asleep in the jail where he is awaiting execution, dreams that his ancestors appear, imploring Jupiter that he be spared; then, after waking up, he finds that a riddle or prophecy has been left by his side; as eventually deciphered by the soothsayer, it puts the seal of divine approval on the play's happy ending. In the world of practical common sense, neither of these elements is at all necessary, or directly functional. Posthumus, detained by the Britons as an enemy, need only declare that he was the soldier in mean attire who fought beside Belarius and the princes to rescue Cymbeline. (As a matter of fact, he has been standing on stage for 330 lines in plain sight of his fellow-combatants, yet unrecognized by them, until he declares himself.) As for the riddle, when once deciphered (it is hardly as deep as a well), it tells the audience nothing more than what it has already seen enacted. Shakespeare rather goes out of his way to show that the intervention of the ancestors comes too late to do any good. Jupiter tells them, crossly enough, not to be so impatient, since he has already decided that

> Your low-laid son our godhead will uplift,
>   His comforts thrive, his trials well are spent. . . .
> He shall be lord of lady Imogen,
>   And happier much by his affliction made.
> (V.iv.103 ff.)

One way of viewing the epiphany is that it serves to explain—if anything like a *deus ex machina* can really explain—gratuitous acts like the decisions to release Posthumus from bondage before it's known who he is and to cancel silently Cymbeline's threat to execute prisoners. On another level, both the vision of the ancestors and the riddle offer relief from the string of explanations and contrite confessions that occupy so much of the last scenes. Both elements elevate the tone of the play's conclusion, which threatens to descend to the mundane, so the intrigues of the characters can be raised to the level of a supernatural concern.

If the play is to rise to splendor, it must be on the strength of a reconciliation between Rome and Britain; for the re-uniting of Posthumus and Imogen (divided only by an obtuse old man and a sneaky trick) and the recovery of the lost princes by Cymbeline (who as a father is less impressive than Belarius) scarcely call for celestial fireworks. But by comparison with the Posthumus-Imogen-Iachimo story, the exposition of the Rome-Britain argument has appeared almost perfunctory. No depth of feeling has entered into it at all (unless perhaps on the part of Cloten, who after his one scene appears to forget all about it). Certainly the audience has no reason to feel anything deeply—what it does feel mildly is that tribute is unwarranted, Caesar being dead, Rome far away, and the historic rationale (protection from barbaric enemies) unmentioned. Lucius has delivered his message civilly, has been received with a profusion of welcomes; Posthumus has served, without moral discomfort, in both armies. No doubt the end of fighting is perceived by the audience as a good thing; but the issue of tribute is neither impressive in itself nor vividly presented. Cymbeline changes his mind about it on what one can only perceive to be a whim and nobody utters a word of protest. For the Olympians to concern themselves with the payment of this petty provincial tax, or to light up the heavens when Cymbeline decides to pay it, seems inordinate.

As a matter of fact, the Rome-Britain dispute has been in real danger of falling out of the middle of the play altogether;

Act III, scene viii looks like a desperate grab to keep it from disappearing. For a brief scene of only 16 lines, Shakespeare transfers us to Rome, where two senators and two tribunes discuss briefly the military situation. The second tribune and the second senator are very secondary indeed; the one says nothing at all, and the other, in response to a question, says wisely, "Ay." Some editors have thrown out the scene entirely, others would transfer it to the last previous scene in Rome, II.v. But apart from weakening the finale of that act (Posthumus' jealous frenzy), moving the senatorial scene from its traditional place would leave the Roman invasion almost unmentioned between III.i and the middle of IV.ii— for nearly a thousand lines of verse, making up eight scenes. (By common computation a hundred lines of verse occupy five minutes of stage time: a thousand lines without mention of the invasion is grotesquely too much.) Awkward as it may be, there is nothing to be done with III.viii except to leave it where it is, and if possible build up the official Roman atmosphere with costumes, props, and some extra business.

Better to conceive of the play's ending, then, as the restoration of a loose and general harmony than as the recovery of cosmic order or the laying-on of hands by one mighty power on another. The least of the public concerns, Imogen's reconcilement with Posthumus, is dramatically the most important. (Psychologically, it also happens to be the shakiest, so the less the characters are allowed to say, the better: if Imogen once turns on Posthumus to utter the fateful words, "You mean to say you actually . . . ?" the whole happy ending shatters like thin crystal.) The political truce, though patently contrived for dramatic convenience, is only *pro forma* anyway, so nobody will be disturbed by it. And the special deep language of both oracle and vision absorbs the audience's attention away from the mere narrative while giving extra validation to the sense of harmony that results.

Two overtones are involved, the inspirational support of the ancestors perhaps deriving from and in any case alluding indirectly to the legend of Scipio's Dream, in which the second great Scipio through a dream is incited to virtue by the spirit of the first. The story of Scipio's dream is hazy, remote, and reaches us only at third hand through the commentaries of Macrobius on a lost passage of Cicero; it is of modern interest mainly as it reveals the outer limits of Cicero's moral cosmology. (As often in neo-Platonic speculations, the question is how close could pagan reason, unaided by Christian faith, come to the creed of the church, and the answer is, Pretty close.) That allusion to the Christian predilections of his audience, distant as it was and dim as they were, is about as close to theology as Shakespeare wanted to come. People who are impressed by the fact that Christ was born during the reign of Augustus, which was also in part the reign of Cymbeline, ought also to be impressed by the fact that Shakespeare neither mentions nor alludes to the fact, even though Holinshed does.* For the playwright, skilled in arts of substitution and implicit analogy, Jupiter and the Genius of the Ancestors came quite close enough to the ultimate divinity.

Another diffusing and refracting lens interposed before the epiphany is the oracle left on Posthumus' sleeping breast. It takes the form—familiar in Shakespeare's time to the point of parody—of a prophecy of Merlin. This legendary Arthu-

---

* To make the moral point of *Cym.* depend on the audience's remembering until the very end of Act V a single phrase from Holinshed of which the author never, even indirectly, put them in mind—from which he actually distracted them with the major businesses of his play—is surely extravagant. That he was too reverent to mention the nativity directly is a logical inversion of the *lucus a non lucendo* variety. Indeed, the characters of *Cym.* pass through distress to content, but so do the central figures of all the other romances; surely a parallel with the transition from the bad old days of paganism to the new dispensation of Christ is not to be sought in all of them.

rian figure was closely associated with the Welsh countryside, and could readily come to mind, even if not mentioned;
already Hotspur knew perhaps too much about him from
the conversation of Glendower. Here his presence, latent
behind the form of a prophetic riddle, joins an indigenous
English with a classical Roman form of visionary insight to
bring about an impressionistic reconcilement of all the rele-
vant auspices. Whether the playwright expected his audience, or the sophisticates among them, to recognize the two
interludes as "skimble-skamble stuff" is an amusing, and not
altogether a trifling, question.

For the dramatic conflict resolved by the two interludes of
Cym. was no out-of-the-way or occasional element in Shakespeare's dramatic career. The deepest chords struck in the
play are those of sexual jealousy—no matter if Posthumus'
complaints reveal elements of pitiful weakness in him, or if
Imogen's submission before Pisanio's sword carries with it a
touch of dubious theatricality. The sexual jealousy that tor-
ments them is no different, generically, than that which constitutes the driving passion in most of the plays, historical
dramas largely excepted, of Shakespeare's previous career.
The man who had written *Hamlet, Othello*, and *Much Ado*
could not have been unaware, when he picked out of the
Decameron story 9 of Day II that he had in hand the natural
materials for yet another tragedy of sexual jealousy. As a
matter of fact, the first four acts of *Cym.* as we now have it
comprise an unbroken series of widening disorders and conflicts, leading to the very verge of bloody disaster. That utter
catastrophe is averted is due to no logic at all, but only to
the unpredictable fluke of Pisanio's disloyal loyalty in refus-
ing to follow orders and kill Imogen. (A play like Tom Stop-
pard's joyous spoof on *Hamlet*, but focussing on the ethical
and emotional dilemmas of Pisanio, could furnish a hilarious
evening's entertainment for playgoers thoroughly familiar

with *Cym*. Among his complaints might be something like, "What am I doing saving the moral bacon of these bloody Brits? I'm nothing but a false, dissembling *Italian!*")

In common language, we would say that Posthumus "embodies" the theme of jealousy, as heroic characters commonly do include in their temper the emotional strain leading to their downfall. But really it's the other way around; jealousy possesses Posthumus, as the bottle is said to ride a drunkard; it almost literally unmans him. But if the theme dominates the character and almost outstretches the play in which it appears, one can hardly expect it to be exorcised by a couple of formulas recited under the shadow of what the audience knows to be the approaching final curtain. In fact, then, Shakespeare might not have minded much our recognizing the end of *Cym*. as skimble-skamble stuff—might have sensed that he had raised in his first four acts more specters than he could conveniently lay in his fifth. To lay them *incon*veniently, then, is a triumph very much in the mode of romance, which not only permits but invites the resolution of insoluble difficulties with a roundelay, a masque, a *deus ex machina*, or a magic show—some device that leaves the audience in a state of surprise, amazement, or, better yet, awe. In addition, it is the nature of Shakespearean themes, even when posed as distinct problems, to mingle with one another over time, so that the solution of one may either imply the solution, or cover the quiet disappearance of some other. Proximity invites a slurring of one concept into the next, a little distance allows changes or reversals. An audience which in III.i thought Cloten a jolly good fellow for talking right back to that Roman stuffed shirt Lucius will accept with equanimity his beheading in IV.ii because he has usurped Posthumus' suit of clothing (ignominy!) and has soliloquized loosely about trying to degrade Imogen. For reasons no higher than these, and often lower, audiences hate or admire stage personages. Political "realities" melt on the stage into sympathy-judgments or dramatic conveniences—a victory, a death, a marriage dynastic or domestic, whatever makes for a strong curtain. The equivocal truce ending the Romano-British war, endorsed by vague formulas from on high, is so necessary to a happy curtain that nobody stops to ask what all those corpses are doing, cluttering up the Welsh landscape.

By a process of fluid interchange, the Shakespearean stage allows one theme to front for another, one sympathy-judgment to crowd past another, one aspect of a character or a concept to blend like the colors on a pigeon's neck imperceptibly into another that suits the playwright's purposes better. "Rome" in the play can stand for empire, for culture, for oppression—it may or may not be contaminated with the "Italian" qualities of decadence, cynicism, and duplicity. "Court" stands for formality and authority but also for softness, "country" for natural affection but also for austere masculine virtue. The associational links tying these elements together may, naturally, be either tight or tenuous, may be recurrent or intimated once and then forgotten. Toward the end of the play, a conclusion is bound to temper all these several energies, with their different permutations, toward one single harmonious chord; and what it cannot fully include or resolve, it at least minimizes or makes inconspicuous.

Trying to lend depth to this synthesizing view of *Cym.*'s ending, we run the risk of introducing incongruous or confusing elements, as with a recent effort to import Orpheus into the play under the guise of Cloten.* More than one Cerberus seems to threaten this enterprise. Cloten is not a loyal husband or a divinely gifted musician; he sings one small song to another man's wife, and she rejects his advances with contempt. He does not adventure into a rec-

* David Armitage, "The Dismemberment of Orpheus," *Shakespeare Survey* 39 (1987).

ognizable underworld to rescue her, for the sufficient reason
that she has not died. For the same reason, he cannot lose
her forever by looking back at her while leaving hell. He is
not torn to pieces by Thracian Maenads either (1) because
he offended Dionysus, or (2) because he drove the ladies
frantic by persuading their husbands to neglect them, or (3)
because they went wild for love of him and his music. The
one point of similarity is that as Orpheus' severed head was
thrown into the Hebrus and carried downstream to the isle
of Lesbos, so Cloten's clotpoll is thrown by Guiderius into
a stream which carries it away, presumably into St. George's
Channel.

There were of course "practical" reasons for disposing de-
cisively of Cloten's head. If Imogen was to mistake the corpse
of Cloten for that of Posthumus (a very sufficient improbability in itself), she could not be allowed to look on its features. A secondary consideration might have been that killing
a man in hand to hand fight and cutting off his head would
suggest to a Jacobean audience primitive warfare and barbaric
customs. A touch of the grisly would not be amiss in this
already fantastic Welsh Arcadia. The princes, perhaps a little
too idealized in their adoration of Fidele, could be given some
authentic country roughness at no cost to anyone the audience cared about. (A loose head rolling and bouncing around
the stage gives more bang for the buck than almost any
equivalent stage property—as anyone will recall who saw the
WPA *Black Macbeth* on the New York stage in the 1930's.)
But inserting two disparate fragments of the Orpheus myth
into the action of *Cym.* just when the presumed Orpheus-
figure has disappeared from the play for good adds incongruous overtones and complications that a common reader
or unindoctrinated audience will have to struggle to elimi-
nate. The whole fifth act could pass by unnoticed, while the
scholarly playgoer sits ruminating in his seat: "What the devil
does this—or that—have to do with Orpheus? Who's Pluto?

Where's Persephone? Where does the snake come in? Is Cloten supposed to be gay?" There's no end to it.*

Of the four romances, *Cym*. contains the least magic—magic in the basic sense of supernatural occurrences or appearances, magic also in the sense of a special conjunction (the heroine and the sea, the newborn baby and the tempest) that Shakespeare used often and apparently with special feeling. In the alluring company of Marina, Perdita, and Miranda, Imogen is rather out of place; she is not of the sea, she is never misplaced for very long, and she is in no sense a wonder or a marvel. For a while in the later 19th century enthusiasts tried to make of Imogen an ideal of wifely purity and devotion. But her rhapsodies to Pisanio on the departure of Posthumus, like her extravagances on the prospect of seeing him again at Milford Haven, are bound to fall rather coldly on modern ears. Perhaps significantly, she comes closest to fulfilling the womanly ideal when she is asleep or "dead." Iachimo, prowling her midnight bedchamber, unfolds a rich tapestry of eloquence on the themes of her beauty, innocence, and luxurious sensual possibilities. Again, the dirge sung over Fidele's "corpse" by the two princes contrasts sharply in its rhythmic and imagistic control with the exclamatory rhetoric that tries to define the attach-

---

* If *Cym*. were an archaeological dig, and one found two shards that between them seemed to depict the story of Orpheus as a single image, they would have to pass many tests before they could be joined. They would have to be made of the same clay, be of the same thickness, painted in the same colors and the same style; they would have to come from the same area and the same temporal stratum; and they would have to fit together along a substantial distinctive lateral surface—not just the irregular edges of the pottery, but the two parts of the design, line for line. When a literary student pulls out of *Cym*. two scraps that might or might not be elements of the Orpheus story, he submits them to no such tests. And they are not scraps dug from a random trashpit, they are units within the organized architecture of a play; they have to fit, not only with each other, but within the complex structure that—one can only hope—has already been recognized.

ment of Imogen and Posthumus to each other. By contrast with those shrill outcries, the dirge moves serenely within itself to reduce its scale of measure. Dismissing the departed soul from the cycles of weather, i.e., nature, the dirge shrinks man's life to a single day, at the close of which he takes his day-wages. The final couplet of the first stanza

> Golden lads and girls all must,
> As chimney sweepers, come to dust,

sounds like a joke or a bit of witty bravado.* Lying down in the grave is a common, an everyday act; black chimney sweepers enter every day into the dark pit, and so must golden boys and girls, however radiant; once there, they are forever secure. "Fear no more" is the keynote of the first three stanzas, and after life's vicissitudes—so the dirge says—there are no others. The dirge ends with a deep wish for "quiet consummation," behind which can perhaps be heard the "consummatum est" of Christ at the end of John's gospel. But Mrs. Dalloway in Virginia Woolf's novel also repeats the key phrase of the dirge as a talisman: "Fear no more," it is a phrase of special sweetness for those who expect neither reward nor punishment, the makeweights of faith.

The dirge's incantatory depth is the major reason for the "magical" feelings surrounding it, even though—far from causing Fidele to stir—it merely deepens the finality of the supposed death. Perhaps it even takes on extra meaning from the fact that Fidele's "death" doesn't serve any apparent narrative function, apart from setting up yet another recognition scene for the last act. If she had not been laid out as a corpse, Imogen could just as easily have stumbled over Cloten's headless corpse by "accident"; her temporary

---

* It's to be noted in passing that the Gaoler's longest speech to Posthumus in V.iv practically recapitulates, in joky terms, the dirge's major theme.

"death" (which might bear some occult significance if it had not been so thoroughly explained [I.vi] by the contrivance and counter-contrivance of the Queen and Cornelius) serves mainly as an occasion for the funeral dirge. It is a terminal poem, to be compared only with the death verses for Thaisa, sinking ever downward through the humming currents of ocean. Though there is nothing in it that transcends the natural, this chant is a moment of magic just as much as any resurrection could be.

The other scene of *Cym.* in which music plays a major role serves mainly to contrast with this one. It is the moment (II.iii) in which Cloten, after a night of dicing and drinking appears before Imogen's casement in the company of some musicians, to serenade her with "Hark, hark, the lark." The performance is encircled by a good many obscene double-entendres on the part of Cloten. He talks of the musicians "penetrating" her with their fingering, and of his trying with his tongue too; he alludes jocularly to the voice of an "un-paved" (i.e., without stones) eunuch. This is quite in line with Cloten's cock-of-the-walk attitude, and suits as well the wake-up-and-sing verses of the lyric he sings; but there is nothing magical or reverberant about it, as Shakespeare has made a point of indicating.

That *Cym.* is sharply different in the matter of magic from the other three romances—all of which not only present more and more explicit magic, but make the action hinge directly on it—is an argument for considering the plays singly rather than as units of a spiritual autobiography. This is not to deny that Shakespeare uses in his plays elements of recurring imagery, as well as units of dramatic action that appear in different guises in different plays. But it's neither possible nor always desirable to find a constant monitory import for these units of business. There are three occasions in *Cym.* for instance, where characters change costume, and in each instance the meaning and circumstances of the change are different. Imogen becomes Fidele as part of a complex but not irrational plot to take service with Lucius and thus get to see Posthumus; Cloten's desire to dress in a suit of Posthumus' clothing in order to disgrace and humiliate Imogen in it is a freak of his wounded pride at her rejection of his advances (II.iii); and Posthumus, about to enter battle, determines to

> disrobe me
> Of these Italian weeds, and suit myself
> As does a Briton peasant.
>
> (V.i)

This is partly symbolic, partly practical; holding himself responsible for Imogen's death, he has no heart to wound Britain further; if he is to fight with the Britons, he must look like one. Putting off Italian weeds (not, emphatically not, Roman armor) may convey a hint of putting off the Iachimo habit of mind; it may further imply the assumption, with humility, of authenticity. Pericles, it's to be recalled, triumphed as "the mean knight"; so does Posthumus "in a silly habit."

From the perspective of the romance tradition some of these episodes can be understood as initiation-tests to which heroes must submit as part of their passage to bliss or illumination. From Apuleius' many humiliations as an ass to Prince Ferdinand's ordeal by logs, it is much the same story. But this rationale doesn't account on any level for Cloten's disguise, nor for Posthumus' humble apparel. If anything, that humble costume should save him from prison and the threat of execution. That it does not is his own deliberate fault. For he is not just a romance hero, but a deeply guilty romance hero. He confesses (falsely) to being a Roman—

inspired, no doubt, by that hunger for death on which the gaoler remarks. Conceivably Shakespeare meant him to pass through the valley of despair before he could be found worthy of, etc. But this line of thought takes us far from his change of garments.

Another thematic veil, which screens out most of the play by providing a grid for part of it, is political allegory. The argument requires one to emphasize Milford Haven as the port where the Earl of Richmond (soon to be Henry VII) landed to claim the throne from Richard III; and to urge a parallel between Cymbeline and James the peacemaker of England. Sometimes the traditional flattering imagery of Stuart masques is adduced to eke out the parallel. But nothing can make the political cross-reference work very well. Even if James did (like Cymbeline) have two sons and a daughter, the sons were never stolen from the nursery, and kept in obscurity for eighteen years; the daughter never disobediently married a commoner. Around the Stuart court there was no conceivable stand-in for Belarius; it would have been a hyper-ingenious playgoer who, looking at the stage figure of Posthumus Leonatus, thought automatically, "Aha! Frederick, the Elector Palatine!" Queen Anne was not much like a witch, and James would not have enjoyed being told she was. He might not, for the matter of that, have enjoyed the representation of himself as a weak old dodderer, despised by his managing wife and obstinate only in his refusal to see merit where everyone else can see it. If indeed James is complimented in *Cym.* as a maker of peace, that compliment is put off to the last minute, when the monarch's pacific intentions are cast into grave doubt by evidence of his weakness and vacillation.

Among the four romances, *Cym.* is uniquely political; it deals with conflicts in the first seed-time of the national destiny, and looks forward to a splendid if cloudy vision of the future. Posthumus, received as Imogen's legitimate husband, is understood to be admitted as well to some sort of informal power-sharing with a reformed Cymbeline, Guiderius, Arviragus, and no doubt—as a steadying adviser—with the faithful Belarius too. As the family circle joins hands, political consensus blossoms, and the play has completed itself.

Practical adjustments have been made, in other words, to some gross imbalances that were felt in the play's early acts. That any of the play's characters have been touched with visionary fire is too much to say. Even Imogen, who has occasioned the play's intermittent bursts of imaginative enthusiasm (Iachimo's gloating, the dirges for Fidele), seems to face little more than a formula future, a "They lived happily ever after" destiny. To the library reader, therefore, *Cym.* is likely to come off as flatter than the other romances. But a resourceful stage production, by assigning the Imogen role to the most bouncy, open-hearted, likable actress available, and by playing up to the maximum patriotic and prophetic elements of Act V, can make of it a thoroughly playable play.

Imaginative dimension may be built out of characters from the inside out (as most notably in the soliloquies of Hamlet) or may be bestowed on them indirectly or directly. In *Per.* Marina-Thaisa-Diana create between them a complex of tremulous relations that aren't strictly part of the characters as made, yet attach to them and enhance their definition. Answering harmonies across attuned distances surround the characters with vibrations. In some of the other romances, one level of existence glimmers into another in a way that makes the audience question its own tangible presence. Sometimes literal characters are able to suggest by their configurations reconciliation on a mythical or visionary level. In *Cym.* one feels this less often, and least often with the central characters. They receive more vibrancies from without than they generate from within or between themselves.

REFERENCES

F. D. Hoeniger, "Irony and Romance in Cymbeline," *Studies in English Literature* XI, no. 2 (Spring, 1962), brings out the discords and incongruities that mark the early stages of the Cymbeline-story, and which come so close to making it a tragedy.

With his usual mixture of astringent irreverence and good sense, G. B. Shaw in *Cymbeline Refinished* rewrote the fifth act of *Cym.*, cutting down on the clutter, converting Imogen to a tough, sensible New Woman, and dismissing both oracle and vision. It's a joyful romp that casts new light on many aspects of Shakespeare's play.

Homer D. Swander, in "Cymbeline: Religious Idea and Dramatic Design," published in *Pacific Coast Studies in Shakespeare*, ed. Waldo McNeir and Thelma Greenfield (Eugene Oregon, 1966), establishes ingenious and persuasive parallels between Cloten and Posthumus in the first part of the play. His efforts to tie the threads of Act V together in terms of the spiritual development of Posthumus are less successful than one could wish them to be.

Emrys Jones, in a review article titled "Stuart Cymbeline," published in *Essays in Criticism* XI, 1 (January, 1961), set forth in part the parallels between the political plot of *Cym.* and the foreign-policy aspirations of James I, which Frances Yates would later develop more extensively and apply more widely in *Shakespeare's Last Plays* (1975).

Making the center of his essay the moment when Imogen wakes beside the headless body of Cloten (but she thinks it is Posthumus), Michael Taylor in "The Pastoral Reckoning in Cymbeline," published in *Shakespeare Survey* 56 (1983), p. 97, proposes it as a consequence of various guilts and faulty attitudes assumed by the lady and her husband—who has, happily, his own penance to perform. The argument is long and strained but at several points illuminating.

Writing on "Cymbeline and the Nativity," in *Shakespeare Quarterly* 13 (1962), p. 207, Robin Moffett makes out a better play structurally than the one Shakespeare wrote. *Non è vero infatti, ma ben trovato.*

IV

THE
WINTER'S TALE

THE TEXT OF *WT* IS FROM THE FIRST FOLIO; THERE WAS NO quarto. Doctor Simon Forman saw a performance at the Globe on May 15, 1611, and recorded in his diary a good summary of the first part of the plot. The saltiers or satyrs who dance at the sheep-shearing festival include (so the servant says) one group of three which "hath danced before the king" (IV.iv.336); there had been a dance of satyrs in Jonson's masque of *Oberon*, produced at court January 1, 1611. But the allusion may not be topical and the dance itself may be a late addition to a play that, in the main, had been written earlier. (Four and a half months seems an improbably short time to write, rehearse, and produce a play of *WT*'s dimensions.)

The source of the story is Robert Greene's *Pandosto*, or, as it is sometimes known from its running title, "The History of Dorastus and Fawnia." Greene's book was first published in 1588 and reprinted in 1592, 1595, and 1607, as well as many times later in the 17th century. Greene himself died in 1592. His novel is in the vein of Greek romances, though specifically indebted, and only in a minor way, only to Longus' *Daphnis and Chloe*. Shakespeare's play borrows or parallels details from a wide range of reading: from Greene's cony-catching pamphlets (about petty street criminals and their dodges), from others of Greene's writings, from Plutarch, from Ovid, from a scattering of old dramas, ballads, and prose narratives, most of which are perhaps-influences. Along with *Tmp.* and a dozen other plays, *WT* was performed at court early in 1613 in connection with the wedding of Princess Elizabeth to Frederick Prince Palatine.

WT begins abruptly; let us imitate it.

Archidamus the guest from Bohemia is in conversation with Camillo the host in Sicilia (I.i). This is a stock way of acclimating an audience at the opening of a play. ("Must be nigh onto twenty years come Michaelmas since young marster left the old homestead." "Aye, I mind, and a bitter cold winter night it was," etc., etc.) Shakespeare had made use of the old formula as recently as *Cym.*, to lay out the rudiments of a situation. But here the exposition doesn't come off very smoothly. Both speakers are lords, royal counsellors, perhaps ambassadors—though without any such titles. Neither in Sicilia nor in Bohemia does there seem to be any very present aristocracy, as of dukes, counts, earls, barons, etc.; no more is there an elaborate apparatus of court officialdom— equerries, chamberlains, heralds, ambassadors. (For that matter, Sicilia seems not to have a senate, a judiciary, or a priesthood—as will become apparent later.) The time is never-never; the play will mingle the Delphic oracle with Whitsun pastorals, artists of the Italian renaissance with roadside foists from English lanes. For the present, Archidamus speaks of "the like occasion whereon my services are now on foot," but defines that occasion and those services no further. Speaking of their respective masters, Camillo explains why, though old friends, they have actually visited

one another very little of late. No doubt Archidamus as a
courtier has understood all this for a long time, but the
audience must be informed. In the first two lines of the
second scene we learn that Polixenes has been at the court
of Sicilia for nine months now, an extended as well as a
suggestive period of time; but Archidamus speaks, and is
spoken to, as a newcomer. Perhaps he has just arrived
from Bohemia, bringing news that all is well in Polixenes'
kingdom: so Hermione seems to say in scene ii, lines
31–32:

> All in Bohemia's well: this satisfaction
> The by-gone day proclaimed.

That would be Archidamus' occasion; but can that have been
all? Does he carry no other message from Polixenes' remarkably reticent, nameless wife,* or from the son to whom
he professes to be deeply attached? Nine months would seem
like a long time, not only to an Elizabethan, but to any
practical statesman, for a king to leave his realm completely
untended; we are never told who's been minding the store.
If Polixenes' queen has nothing to say to her husband after
all this time but "All's well," it's a matter for remark; if she
has ventured to say to her husband, though never so mildly,
that his return would be welcome one of these days, that
too might come up in the edgy, over-mannered argument of
scene ii about whether he is to stay or go. Nothing of the
sort rises to the surface. After his few lines in this first scene
of all, Archidamus disappears from the play for good.

---

* In *Pandosto* the nameless wife of Egistus king of Sicilia is daughter to the
emperor of Russia; the alliance puts Egistus beyond Pandosto's revenge.
In *WT* the wife of Polixenes, still nameless, is deprived of her pedigree
as well, to enrich Hermione, strongly defined as wife, as mother, and as
an emperor's imperial daughter.

Whether he actually saw Polixenes, and what he said to him, are left to our conjecture. What he is doing with Camillo is very much beside all the practical points; they have no business to discuss, only compliments to bandy back and forth. For Archidamus has never been to Sicilia before, he is overwhelmed by the lavishness of his entertainment, and that is the theme of their talk. Camillo makes nothing of it ("You pay a great deal too dear for what's given freely") but Archidamus strains his vocabulary to express his gratitude and his imagination to conceive a fitting response. Both interlocutors speak the language of courtly compliment, but Camillo commands it with far greater suavity and dexterity than poor Archidamus, who stutters and falters in the effort to keep up:

> Verily I speak it in the freedom of my knowledge: we cannot with such magnificence . . . in so rare . . . I know not what to say.
>
> (I.i.11 ff.)

"Verily" is one of those telltale milk-and-water asseverations that Shakespeare often ridiculed; it will be held up to mockery within the first act of this play. Through Archidamus only (and therefore only in this scene) do we get a sense that Bohemia, though perhaps a powerful kingdom, is by contrast with Sicilia an unsophisticated and downright provincial one. The Bohemians' only way of entertaining the Sicilians, when they pay the promised counter-visit, will be to make their friends so drunk they won't recognize the inadequacy of their entertainment. Germanic countries traditionally took a more tolerant view of drunkenness than Latin ones; it is a notion made explicit, for example, in Erasmus' "Julius Exclusus." Shakespeare could be touching on it here, if only as a cliché familiar to his audience. But perhaps also in view of Archidamus' less urbane diction and ruder notions of entertainment, he thought of Bohemia as a more natural and genuine society—less sophisticated than Italy but more authentic. The flavor of such a contrast is very strong indeed in *Cym.*; it may have carried over here, with Bohemia a kind of transposed England, Sicilia a surrogate Italy. Considerations of this general nature might explain why *WT* reverses the locales of *Pandosto*: events which in Greene's romance occur in Bohemia are transferred in Shakespeare's play to Sicilia and vice versa.

For no immediate reason, talk turns to Leontes' son, prince Mamillius. Archidamus, though but newly arrived, has seen him and praises him, actually speaking in the process his curious name.* It compounds a diminutive *-lillus* with the word for mother, *mama*, or perhaps breast, *mamma*. Mamillius, as we will learn, is quite a little boy, not yet beyond the need to have his nose wiped for him, still the plaything of his mother's maids; but Archidamus pays him a more than generous compliment—"a gentleman of the greatest promise that ever came into my note." The audience has not yet seen Mamillius, or for that matter his parents, and cannot therefore anticipate what sort of gentleman this will be; but it is given two widely disparate indications: a gentleman of supreme promise not too far removed from the nipple. There is a wide open space in between. But Camillo, not satisfied with the compliment, must build his own structure of fatuous praise:

> it is a gallant child; one that indeed physics the subject, makes old hearts fresh; they that went on crutches ere he was born desire yet their life to see him a man.
>
> (I.i.37 ff.)

---

* Besides *Pandosto* (1588), from which the main plot of *WT* derives, Robert Greene wrote a romance, *Mamillia* (1583); in a play that includes an insouciant "snapper-up of unconsidered trifles," it doesn't seem insignificant that Shakespeare should be borrowing such trifles boldly from the work of a man who had once accused him of plagiarism.

The hyperbole is piled a little too high for the common sense of Archidamus: he turns on his host. "Would they else be content to die?" he asks, and, brushing aside Camillo's silly evasion, concludes with blunt realism, "If the king had no son, they would desire to live on crutches till he had one."

The conversation has bottomed out with a bump on the hard ground of common sense. "Let us e'en talk a little like folk of this world"—it is Falstaff's down-to-earth English phrase, and it speaks to Archidamus' condition as outsider. The scene is an index, though the directions in which it points can be seen only in aftersight. Even with the help of aftersight, it may seem to point at overlapping targets, perhaps at a court-country contrast, or the differences between yokel Bohemia and artificial Sicilia (with overtones of England and Italy), perhaps at the old polarity between nature and artifice. It may imply a thrust at over-supple Camillo, whose part in the play as the trustworthy untrustworthy will be not unlike that of Pisanio in *Cym*. It may strike at flattery or the stilted dialect of a coterie. By indirection, it may suggest that the king within whose court this sort of talk passes current has been subject to a good deal of stroking.

The artifice of that court-dialect in which most of the first three acts are framed invites special attention. Polixenes begins:

> Nine changes of the wat'ry star hath been
> The shepherd's note, since we have left our throne
> Without a burthen.
>
> (I.ii.1 ff.)

What looks like the subject of the sentence turns out, after the first six words, to be a predicate noun and in its force not far from a direct object; a prosaic paraphrase of the sentence, reduced to its common English word order, would be, "The shepherd has celebrated nine times the cycle of the moon." "Hath," which is a singular form, goes more naturally with "note" than with "changes"; though Shakespeare is not always meticulous about this sort of numerical agreement, still Polixenes' sentence floats between two grammars. Just as delicately, it alludes, but only equivocally, to "The Shepherd's Calendar"; as the idea of "months" flowers out of the locution "changes of the wat'ry star," so "calendar" blossoms out of the allusive idea of "months." The assertion dances, as it were, on a narrow associative verge behind the actual words of the script; one catches at them as they pass, or even afterwards—part of the game is catch-up. As for the conclusion of the sentence, it is striking that the king of Bohemia actually speaks of an inanimate object, the throne, lacking a dead weight, himself—not of royal duties to be performed, a family needing its father, or anything else involving people. This is courtly deference with a vengeance. The first principle of this dialect is distance; the audience isn't kept in suspended doubt about what is being said, but it has to wait for the sentence to complete itself grammatically, then look back a ways and transpose, transfer, meta-phore. The hearer, in brief, is suspended by the ear.

Syntactical high-jinx abound in court speech; they are the common dialect. Hermione replies to her husband's frantic charges with a sentence which, between ellipses and inversions and changes of grammatical direction, takes more than a little decipherment:

> More than mistress of
> Which comes to me in name of fault, I must not
> At all acknowledge.
> (III.ii.59 ff.)

The full prosaic sense would be, "I must not at all acknowledge (myself to be) mistress of more than (that) which is fairly imputed to me as a fault." Even so eked out, the construction "mistress of a fault" remains strained, and the "more than" which in the text seems to apply to "mistress" turns out in logic to apply to the half-elliptic "(that) which." One doesn't greatly overstate in saying that the sentence is given to us in elegant disarray which our minds after a moment reassemble. So, for a final example, with a speech in which Leontes confesses that he had wanted to poison his good friend Polixenes—

> which had been done,
> But that the good mind of Camillo tardied
> My swift command, though I with death, and with
> Reward, did threaten and encourage him,
> Not doing it, and being done.
>
> (III.ii.161 ff.)

The six elements string together in two chains of three: death-threaten-not doing and reward-encourage-being done; but the complicating fact remains that "reward" and "threaten" stand beside one another, implying juncture, as do "encourage" and "not doing it." At the end, active and passive participles stand in contrast, the subjects only implied—(his) doing it, and (it) being done, with the additional complication that one has to dissociate words that seem by proximity to attract one another.

Intricate and sometimes flashy word play is frequently considered a general characteristic of later Shakespeare, and even made a basis for dating the plays; but within *WT* at least, the playwright seems more concerned to make it an expression of character or of social position. Rural personages, including Autolycus with his mixed background, Paulina and Antigonus, and very strikingly indeed the oracle (famed as a rule for veiled, ambiguous judgments) make use of the simple, direct idiom. If a contrast is developed within the play, it can hardly be unrelated to the blunt force of the first scene. Indeed, Camillo seems to be a crucial instance in the counterpoint of fine words and flat facts. Though consistently labelled "honest," and given to asserting things on his "honor," he is not, in the moment of crisis, much of a paragon. After feigning docile obedience to Leontes, he easily moves to conniving at the escape of Polixenes, while barely considering the fate to which he is abandoning Hermione; after promising to help Florizel against his father's bilious rage, he instantly goes back on his promise, and for the least loyal of reasons, his own desire to see Sicily again. Indeed, he had previously protested a little against the jealous rage of Leontes, but not much; against the fury of Polixenes he protests not at all. By contrast with Paulina (to whom he is abruptly, wordlessly united by royal edict at the play's last gasp), Camillo has asserted no presence at all. In talking to Florizel, he has been quite lavish in promises to placate the king—

> with my best endeavors in your absence
> Your discontenting father strive to qualify
> And bring him up to liking.
>
> (IV.iv.531 ff.)

But the play provides no reason to think he has done anything of the sort; nor, given his basic motivation, getting back to Sicily, has he any impulse to do so. If he persuades Polixenes to look kindly on the marriage of Florizel and Perdita, the play will end practically, undramatically, prematurely in Bohemia, with an "All is forgiven, come home at once" message.

Behind the dallying of his puppets, the playwright's own interests have to be observed here. He has to get his cast back to Sicily so the double revelation of Perdita's birth and Hermione's preservation can burst on the two kings (and the

audience) in a climactic *coup de théâtre*. We are in fact given
every reason to think Hermione dead. Apart from Paulina's
vehement words announcing the fact, Antigonus' description
(III.iii) of the vision in which her ghost appeared to him
should have removed every doubt from an audience's mind.
On the other hand, Shakespeare must have known from the
beginning that his play could not end, like *Pandosto*, with
Hermione in her grave and Leontes a suicide atop it. Other
considerations apart, that scene might have cast a bit of a
pall over the happy marriage of Perdita and Florizel. Accordingly, Antigonus' dream must be a deliberate piece of
authorial indirection, a setup for the amazing, and even incredible, reversal of Act V.

Shakespeare commonly manipulates his audience in this
way, though not often so openly. Throughout the play, artifice, omission, and indirection are used to prevent softening
or premature disclosure of the action. Thus Camillo, despite
his promises to the prince, does nothing to placate Polixenes,
while Autolycus, for reasons which are no reasons, distracts
Clown and Shepherd on their way to tell the king about
Perdita's mysterious birth. Both fall in the general category
of Shakespearean interferers and delayers (like Dogberry and
Verges of *Much Ado*); but the contrast between them is
pointed. Camillo, though a man of some rank and preten-
sions to honor, directly and unhesitatingly betrays his word
given to Florizel; while Autolycus, a professional thief and
deceiver, refuses to snitch on the eloping lovers, citing
professional ethics, no less:

> If I thought it were a piece of honesty to acquaint the
> king withal, I would not do't: I hold it the more knav-
> ery to conceal it, and therein am I constant to my
> profession.

> (IV.iv.680 ff.)

This is a curious way to phrase the matter because the same
point could be put the other way around, and more flatter-
ingly to himself. Autolycus was formerly servant to Prince
Florizel, and he is not (it appears) without hankerings to
resume his former livery. What he has done in keeping the
prince's secret could be represented as loyalty to the prince
no less naturally than as treachery to the king. In this ticklish
matter of truth and loyalty, Autolycus as honest rogue—and
self-confessed rogue at that—takes most of the points from
Camillo the deceitful man of "honor" who seems not to know
which master he is serving. Including the play's first scene,
this will be the second time that Camillo compares unfavor-
ably with a plainer man or one less acceptable socially. In
other forms, this is an old contrast in Shakespearean drama;
the bard had a standing fondness for rascals, roughnecks,
and knowing innocents. Autolycus, however, is a distinctive
blend.

He enters the play from nowhere in particular, and departs
in the same direction; he is detached and utterly unpredictable. His name is that of a son of Hermes, father of Anticlea
and thus grandfather of Odysseus; it appears in *Odyssey* XIX
in connection with the story of Odysseus' scar, also in *Metamorphoses* XI, lines 360–64 of Golding's translation. But that
is not where he comes from; neither does he come from
Greene's *Pandosto*, though an ordinary courtier named Capnio does perform several of Autolycus' actions in the play,
i.e., encouraging the lovers to make their getaway and di-
verting Shepherd and Clown on board the ship. But Capnio
is only the smallest fraction of Autolycus. His tricks as pick-
pocket, ballad-seller, and quick-change artist come from
Greene's cony-catching pamphlets, and the notion of applying to him the classical name "Autolycus" must be the work
of a wide-reaching ironic imagination that we cannot apply
to anyone so properly as to Shakespeare himself. It is a

deliberate authorial intrusion on the texture of the play; Autolycus is the most contemporary and present figure in the narrative—journalistic in his immediacy, yet with the most ancient and mythological of names. (He would be "Jemmy Twitcher" or "Three-Fingered Matt" in so-called real life.) Where he came from is less of a question than what he is doing in the play. At first, he is simply a figure of mischief and fun. Stealing from the Clown, selling ballads and baubles to country simpletons while picking pockets, he provides a most elegant obbligato of low realism in the world of pastoral poetry. But when he interferes in the elopement of Florizel and Perdita (abetted, so they suppose, by Camillo), the activities of Autolycus become more puzzling.

He is, for example, taken without question or hesitation into Camillo's scheme for disguising the runaways—a mad scheme in itself, since it is designed to elude a merely suppositious pursuit, and involves as its very first step taking in an unknown and obviously untrustworthy accomplice. Though the change of clothes with Florizel fulfills to some extent Autolycus' reputation from antiquity as a quick-change artist, it leads to no consequences, good or bad; no more does Autolycus' subsequent diversion of Clown and Shepherd from their errand to the king. He leads them off to the prince's ship, to be sure; but there, though eager to prove themselves unrelated to Perdita, and possessed of all the necessary proofs, they are incapable of conveying the fact to anyone in the course of their journey from Bohemia to Sicily. Meanwhile Autolycus somehow and for no defined reason makes the same trip aboard the king's ship without revealing anything to Polixenes or arousing the suspicion of Camillo, who has known him previously only as a convenient ragamuffin. At the court of Leontes, Autolycus, though apparently present at the great reconciliation-scene, is not allowed to describe more than a small fraction of it, his mouth being stopped by a couple of nameless "gentlemen." Shakespeare leaves his ultimate disposition curiously indeterminate in a practical way, though suggestive symbolically.

In short, though Autolycus has many appearances, he is a most insubstantial piece of dramatic substance, whose mockery of simple shepherdesses, in his repeated transparent assurances to Mopsa and Dorcas that the ballads he is peddling are "true" seems on the surface too easy and almost pointless. The girls are anxious for reassurance on the point of "truth"; he vouches lavishly for the most outlandish absurdities, and uses the occasion to filch purses. His business is illusion; so is his nature. (He is not an allegory of deceit, he is deceit itself.) That name of his, which advertises and at the same time conceals his nature, rings sweet discord on the contemporary thieves' lingo in which he brags of his doxies and his aunts. To a remarkable degree, he is inconsequential; the money he steals is hardly missed, the ballads he sells are no sooner believed than forgotten, the stuff in his pack exists only to be sung about and sold. He relates less closely to the characters in the story than to the story as seen from without.

Many years ago, in a collection of more or less theoretical essays, I suggested that Autolycus might fairly be identified with the capricious Shakespearean fancy; I meant, though I wasn't bold enough to say it, with Shakespeare himself as a figure in and behind the playhouse. And I still find acceptable the notion that in Autolycus we have an instance, exceptional mainly in its pointedness, of Shakespeare larking with his entire relation to the theater. Like Autolycus with the Clown, he is picking the pocket of the departed Robert Greene; like Autolycus with Dorcas and Mopsa, he is peddling ridiculous stories to simple-minded citizens; like Autolycus he is liberated both from the stodgy codes of respectability and from the insistence of dull innocents that they be told at every stage "the truth." In Shakespeare's earlier plays there are hints and partial foreshadowings of such an attitude, as in *A Midsummer Night's Dream* and *Antony and Cleopatra*, where mockery of stage appearances is used to suggest a more precious imaginative reality withdrawn behind the mere representation. Here in the person of Autolycus Shakespeare gives away the whole show to anyone witty enough to get his point. But the giveaway is a statement that even when the whole apparatus of story, characters, scenery, theater, and the shabby exchange of shillings is cast down, some transcendent imaginative reality will remain. The joy that suffuses the capering, evanescent figure of Autolycus counts, one might think, among the better indications that the last four plays are suffused with a visionary spirit, not religious or mystical but nonetheless celebratory. Reading the character as a common transgressor against property rights, who gets his come-uppance when he is made to exchange a few subservient words with the freshbaked "gentlemen born" of V.2, is to enlist onself with Mopsas and Dorcases of this world.

Leontes' reconciliation with Perdita and Florizel's atonement with Polixenes have been criticized as dramatically weak because narrated at second hand or even passed over altogether rather than enacted before the audience. But Shakespeare could not have three recognition-reconcilement scenes piled one atop the other at the end of his play. In letting the recovery of Hermione stand as by synecdoche for the others, he chose a scene in which music combines with the simplest of gestures and a minimum of words to create a sense of awe, release, and separation in the very act of coming together. The wonderful melts here into the inexplicable; the story does not end, it dissolves. The very framework of the situation is preposterous. Hermione has lived as in a tomb for sixteen years, during which her passionately repentant husband has daily visited her grave, yearning to have her back; yet she has remained silent, unmoved. Why?

Better not ask. It's a mystery, veiled and irrational as a dream, and as little to be questioned. But the shakier the burial-resurrection of Hermione is as a practical action, the richer it is as a Demeter-Persephone ritual, casting a magic-lantern image behind Leontes as an analogue of gloomy Dis, who ripped the maiden from her mother's arms, and carried her off to the fiery darks of the underworld.

Classical analogies in WT have to be handled with utmost gentleness, partly because they are built into the culture and so can scarcely be avoided, partly because Shakespeare mutes, conceals, and distances them in a variety of ways to be described, so that they come together for the most part retrospectively. In the course of the first three acts, Perdita never advances beyond infancy, and her utter rejection by Leontes seems like an antithesis to the abduction of Proserpina by Dis. The locale of Leontes' court in Sicilia is not stressed; Hermione's pregnancy is presented without the hint of a mythological overtone. Proserpina is not directly mentioned till the sheep-shearing scene, when it is Perdita herself who speaks the name, applying it then to "maidens" whose innocence we have sampled in the hoydens Mopsa and Dorcas. Proserpina is related to spring and the return of fertility to the land, but Perdita's relation to the changing seasons is carefully shaded. Sheep-shearing is an event of the late spring, but Perdita says she wishes she had some flowers of the spring for Florizel and the girls—what she has to hand for Polixenes and Camillo are flowers of winter, softened by her courtesy to flowers of middle summer. By these several indirections, and others like them, classical parallels are intimated gently, toned down, left behind as the action of the play advances, but roused again by resonances in the later parts of the action, especially the dénouement.

Thus the "strong scene" at the end of the play—tears, shrieks, vows, embracings—absence of which has been deplored, was exactly what Shakespeare didn't want and contrived to avoid. From the beginning he made clear, and repeatedly reminded his audience, that his fable was idle, empty, a mere pastime. That didn't mean there was nothing to the play; on the contrary, it was an invitation to drop the story and look for the imaginative meaning within it. An imaginative meaning, that is, not a didactic or allegorical one. The Shakespeare characters do not "stand for" agents in another sphere of reference or on another plane of reality. His characters have no fixed essence; at any given point they are what the action of the play's language makes them; and if in the concluding scene of *WT* they seem thin, that may be because then for the first time tonalities half-sounded earlier in the play have been drawn together to produce a chord that their mere human natures, too thick or too profuse, would mute.

Nature is an elusive and various presence in this elusive and various play. As he sends the Clown and the Shepherd along to Florizel's (inexplicably) waiting ship and their (wholly unanticipated) trip to Sicilia,* Autolycus pauses a moment to look upon the hedge and soliloquize. His soliloquy does not tell the audience anything it did not already know, and his sending the two yokels ahead, unaccompanied, to explain to the runaways business that really lies with the king, makes little practical sense. The important "secrets" lie in the fardel, and the Clown, with his usual verbal generosity, has already given away most of them: " 'tis none of your daughter or my sister." This opens many possibilities which a man of Autolycus' quick wit could profit by exploring or explaining to anyone in authority; yet he hangs back, to answer a call of nature. Indeed, this euphemism is quite as appropriate as the one he actually uses. To "look upon the

---

* In *Pandosto* the shepherd Porrus is forcibly snatched onto Dorastus' ship; there is no figure equivalent to Shakespeare's clown, i.e., the shepherd's son.

hedge" is to urinate, and this Autolycus presumably does onstage, as he soliloquizes, with a degree of discreetness that's up to the actor. The scene is unique in the plays of Shakespeare.

Is "answering the call of nature" the point of the performance? As a vagabond and a man on the outs with the law, Autolycus is the very character to violate proprieties, including dramatic decorums. But what for him is just one more piece of gratuitous impudence is quite another thing for a playwright intent on honing the fine edge of a dramatic illusion. Perhaps Shakespeare was not so intent. Or perhaps he calculated that breaking a common convention of the stage was a way to strengthen the illusions not broken, to make them seem more real. Whatever the way of it, the episode of Autolycus and the hedge is only one of many in which the playwright deliberately lowered and vulgarized the precious tone of *Pandosto*. He excised ruthlessly, for instance, the operatic soliloquies in which Greene's characters took frequent opportunity to indulge: "Infortunate Fawnia and therefore infortunate because Fawnia," etc., etc. He introduced the Clown, Perdita's supposed brother, of whom Greene never thought, and made him a true Shakespearean bumpkin-wit, a predestined victim for such as Autolycus, broad of speech and enthusiastic for bawdy ballads. (Yet he is not altogether a dummy, either; those who smile at his simplicity should try doing in their heads the calculation on which he is first engaged: "every 'leven wether tods, every tod yields pound and odd shilling: fifteen hundred shorn— what comes the wool to?")* In parts of the play far removed from yokelry and peasant dialect, Paulina is another of Shakespeare's natural contributions to the narrative, not very far removed from the character of Emilia in *Othello*, and like Emilia vehement and fearless in speaking her heart. She

* The answer is, approximately, 143 pounds six shillings.

speaks not only her own nature, but for the natural feelings; to be in touch with nature of this sort, no less than communing with the birds and flowers, is to be authentic. (I mean, of course, stage-authentic, nothing more.) The dialect of Paulina (and to a lesser extent of Antigonus), the puppy-smut of the Clown, and the vagabond spatterings of Autolycus, all stand out (as needs no emphasis) from the artful hyperbole and duplicitous formalities of polite court society. They are all original Shakespeare contributions to the story. Looking backwards, the homely dialect of the Pentapolitan fishermen in *Per.* and the gallows-familiarities of Posthumus' gaoler in *Cym.* appear to be woven of the same stuff.

Profuse and indiscriminate, nature provides a nature to vouch for everything, yet she is hedged in by conventions that are at least second nature. Why shouldn't classes intermarry as plants are cross-bred? Polixenes can see the sense of the latter process, though not of the former; the audience no doubt catches the irony, but it's an easy and superficial one. The play itself, knowing something of audience expectations and standards of satisfaction, remains aloof. Though Perdita, defending herself against the aspersions of the angry king, reminds the audience that

> The selfsame sun that shines upon his court
> Hides not his visage from our cottage, but
> Looks on alike—
>
> (IV.iv.445 ff.)

this is a very dubious, theoretical equality. The daughter of royalty, Perdita is instinctively, *naturally*, recognized as superior to her humble adopted environment. By genetic inheritance, presumably, she talks a different dialect than her "brother" and his playmates Dorcas and Mopsa. Though the audience bravely agrees, for the moment, that the sun shines on rich and poor alike, it would not be satisfied if this peerless

piece of earth married a common shepherd-clown. It will not
be satisfied until, recognized socially as an authentic princess, she is united with her "natural" social equal, an authentic prince, who has proved his "natural" passion for her
by being willing to forego his princedom. Thus several different and contrasting natures are gratified at once.

In passing, one notes that the four invented but "natural"
characters through whom Shakespeare brought on stage different accents of authentic speech or less than courtly behavior, though disposed of casually, depart each with a comic
barb. Paulina, who has demonstrated talents as a stage manager, is put in charge of Camillo; this looks like just another
convenient pre-curtain coupling, but may also carry the connotation that the sharpness of her tongue will be needed to
curtail the excessive suppleness of his. Another odd couple
forms up in the shadows. The Clown having declared himself
a gentleman born, his state is, as he very wisely says, "preposterous," and he is in a position to vouch for the character
of his new friend Autolycus. They march off together. The
world has turned upside down as well as back to front, and
it seems to work very well that way. Knave and fool reach
an agreement that parodies, or perhaps simply parallels, the
alliances of the upstairs gentry. In its straightfaced levity this
droll demarche aligns with such earlier semi-jocose elements
as the demise of Antigonus on the stormy, and bear-infested,
seacoast of Bohemia. It isn't just the basic spoof elements of
this story, but the over-excited hilarity of the Clown in describing it—the scenes of chaotic violence presented as grotesquely funny—that make the flavor of the play particularly
wry at this juncture. Shakespeare, by choosing to see the
end of Act III, the shipwreck and its consequences, through
the excitable, fantastic eye of the Clown, seems deliberately
to deny sympathy just where straight dramatic emphasis
would seem to call for most of it.

The drowning of the crew is nothing. No doubt they all

had traits, but a theater audience with an economy of sympathy to apportion out, can be trusted to forget all about them in twenty seconds. The eating alive—and piecemeal—of Antigonus is another matter because in his encounters with Leontes and in his care for Perdita he had earned a measure of liking, even trust. His death is a practical necessity; he cannot be left around to tell stories about Perdita's origins (and so give away the end of the play) at the court of Polixenes. Getting rid of him violently and jocosely at the same time leaves the audience with two conflicting emotions that cancel each other out. The straightfaced levity of this central instant says something about the quirky nature of the action as a whole. "I love a ballad but even too well," the Clown has declared, "if it be doleful matter merrily set down; or a very pleasant thing indeed and sung lamentably." An audience could hardly expect fairer warning; the imp of the perverse is at loose in the comedy.

Though king Leontes' abrupt, unmotivated rage in the first act of *WT* has been amply criticized as a deficiency in the play, not so much attention has been paid to the abrupt, unmotivated rage of king Polixenes in Act IV. In fact, *Pandosto* provides both monarchs with ample motivation. Bellaria in Greene's novel comes close to playing fast and loose with her royal guest; Greene slyly tempts us into thinking it likely. And Egistus' fury with his son Dorastus flares up for reasons that Elizabethans would have found instantly familiar; the father had arranged a marriage for his son with an heiress (Euphrania princess of Denmark), and was not going to see it disrupted by an affair with a common shepherdess. But Shakespeare made no effort to provide credible motives for Leontes/Pandosto, and discarded the motive that Greene had already provided for Polixenes/Egistus. Lacking the sort of specific motivation that would distinguish them, the two kinds meld practically indistinguishably into identical mechanisms of suspicion, sullen repression, and abrupt fury bursting out into fantastic threats of burning, mutilation, and bloody execution.

If the kings are twin bogeys, setting the two halves of the plot into motion, they play little part in the reconciliation. In the course of Act V, Leontes never addresses to his daughter a word that the audience can hear, nor does Polixenes say a word to his son; in fact, Leontes addresses only a brief sentence to Bohemia, perfunctorily begging pardon for his scandalous suspicions and his efforts to murder a sacred guest as well as a dear friend. It occurs in the last ten lines of the play, and is needed no doubt; but its implications are colder even than silence, for it shows that in the time they have been together (whatever it may be) Leontes has not yet begged pardon, a speech that ought to have been on the tip of his tongue at their first meeting. Thus, for whatever reason, the true climax of that last scene rises from the reunion of mother and daughter. Only after Perdita, doing worship to her mother as a sacred image, violates a taboo deeply rooted in the audience's mind (though absurdly irrelevant to her own supposed culture), is Hermione released to human speech. Perdita, speaking half to the onlookers on stage, half to the audience, says,

> And give me leave,
> And do not say 'tis superstition, that
> I kneel and then implore her blessing.
>
> (V.iii.42 ff.)

Her precautionary phrase, implying as background an accumulation of propaganda against the worship of images, invites us to suppose some supernatural spirit behind or within the image made by Julio Romano. Apart from the fable of Pygmalion and Galatea and a long tradition of critical talk about "breathing images," an Elizabethan audience, given a play with a semi-classical setting, might have contributed on its own thoughts of an immanent Genius, sprite, spirit of vital sympathy, or mythical patroness, capable of rousing Hermione to life. No doubt such mythical explanations impose more strain on an audience's credulity than would a "natural" one, as we sense from Paulina's effort to redress the balance:

> That she is living,
> Were it but told you, should be hooted at
> Like an old tale
> (V.iii.115 ff.)

The logic is contorted, and characteristic enough of the poet, to merit a moment. That she (the boy-actor personating Hermione) is living, we can see; if we were told the real reasons why she (the character in the play) is living after sixteen years of seclusion, we would think them incredible—why not then (by tacit implication) accept the mythical or supernatural explanation, which is no more improbable? This pattern of linking the unfamiliar (but true) with the purely fabulous to the conclusion that both must be perfectly believable is repeated in *Tmp.* when old Gonzalo tries to settle Alonso's fears about spirits:

> When we were boys,
> Who would believe that there were mountaineers
> Dew-lapp'd like bulls, whose throats had hanging at
> 'em
> Wallets of flesh? or that there were such men
> Whose heads stood in their breasts?
> (III.iii.43 ff.)

You wouldn't believe A if I told you, so you might as well believe B because after all D is right before your eyes. In the interval of stunned silence while this cats'-cradle is being untangled, the story of Julio Romano quietly dwindles to just another piece of hocus-pocus.

At the end of Greene's novel, king Pandosto—overwhelmed with guilt at having killed his wife and son, and lusted after his daughter—commits suicide. That leaves Bohemia without a ruler, enabling Fawnia and her new husband Dorastus to ascend the throne without hesitation. To be sure, the prophecy of the oracle is not very well fulfilled by this solution, for the king does not live after his heir is discovered; but oracles are apt to be tricky in matters like this.* A further inconvenience is that Dorastus, legitimate heir of Egistus, is taken away from Sicilia to be king of Bohemia. But, given the shortage of eligible males after the death of Garinter/Mamillius, this is inevitable; whichever kingdom gets the pair of young lovers, the other kingdom will be left without an heir. And in fact Shakespeare, who did not have an empty throne to fill (having decided to keep Leontes alive), solved the problem in his usual tactful, indefinite manner, by declining to indicate whether Perdita and Florizel would live henceforth in Sicilia or Bohemia. Dynastically, the situation is worse than precarious; one can imagine Leontes and Polixenes—both testy, impatient monarchs—locking horns over where the children are to live and what kingdom they are to rule over. But this, like most other literal, practical dilemmas, overlooks the fact that the marriage is primarily a conventional sign.

Mythologically, the reuniting of Proserpina with Ceres is the renewal of nothing less than the world; it is the restoration of fertility, an escape from death. When the maiden is

---

* Somebody felt the force of this objection, because in the 1607 and later editions of *Pandosto*, the oracle is made to say "the king shall *die* without an heir." Forman reported the words of the oracle as "die without yssue," and that, as a stronger prophecy, may have been what the actor said. But the play, like the edition of *Pandosto* Shakespeare was following, says unmistakably "live."

freed from her underground prison, if only for a season, the world in general is freed from sterility. Perhaps Leontes and Hermione will blossom anew. Perhaps Florizel (pallid as an individual like Lysimachus of *Per.*) will provide the monarchs with an overplus of scions. Perhaps the oracle, since it never specified *which* king would recover his heir, felt its prophecy would be fulfilled by Polixenes' recovery of Florizel—though, as Florizel has never really been lost, that solution seems like a cop-out. By whatever means, whether by some dispensation of nature's laws or device of verbal avoidance, the audience leaves the theater feeling that basic difficulties have been overcome. Just as the Clown, without effort, has become a gentleman born, muddling deliciously the question of which is his second nature and which his first—just as Autolycus, though not naturally honest, is so sometimes by chance, and that is enough—so Sicilia and Bohemia, we feel, will find heirs when heirs are needed. Nature vouches for the fact, in that one season succeeds another, inevitably; Time himself has appeared on stage, saying, very *à propos*,

> let Time's news
> Be known when 'tis brought forth.
> (IV.i.26 f.)

Temporis filia veritas is a better motto for Shakespeare's play than for Greene's novel, where it actually appears. Two hours have passed in the playhouse, the same two hours for all the audience, their passage thus confirmed by common experience. Time has made a personal appearance on stage, dressed no doubt in toga and sandals, with the shaggy locks and fierce scythe that he inherited from his cannibalistic predecessor Saturn/Chronos. His appearance marks a turning point; in the first part of the play, he has acted as a destroyer, in the fourth and fifth acts he will be seen as the revealer of truth unjustly obscured. As Saturn, he is no less associated

with Sicilia than Proserpina and her abductor Dis; the plain
of Leontium, just north of modern Lentini, is not only where
the god of the underworld disappeared with his victim but
where the scythe of Saturn (which can also be considered
the scythe of Ceres) lies hidden. These connections are made
by Natalis Comes, II.2 "De Saturno" and V.14 "De Cerere";
that king Leontes got his name from the "planitie Leontia"
is only a speculation, but it could add to a pattern.

Bringing Time on stage to fill a gap in the construction
looks back in a way to the choral figure of Gower in *Per.*
and to the Chorus of *Henry V*. But both previous instances
are natural (so to speak) playhouse figures; neither is an
abstract noun masquerading as a person. It's dubious that
in coopting Time for a brief spot in his play, Shakespeare
intended any major metaphysical overtones; but such a figure, coming from so far outside the story and making so
little effort to fill it in as a story, cannot help strengthening
the play's sense of artifice. As a matter of fact, Time tells us
more of himself as a universal builder and destroyer than he
does about the progress of the tale, which he mentions only
to say that nothing has happened to Leontes while Florizel
and Perdita have been growing up. The first lines of the
Polixenes-Camillo scene following Time's prologue inform us
again that fifteen years have passed, that prince Florizel exists, and that he is starting to take a particular interest in
Perdita. With only a very few verbal adjustments to that
scene between Polixenes and Camillo, Shakespeare (had he
chosen to) could have obviated altogether the occasion for
Time and his speech. The fact that he chose not to do so
indicates, evidently, that he wanted to emphasize, not
bridge, the gap between Act III and Act IV. Intervention of
a supernal force like Time has a further effect of diminishing
the stature and autonomy of the play's characters; they are
seen as little people moving around the floor of the world
under the influence of powers beyond their control or un-

derstanding. To a degree, this is a common characteristic of the romances; when Florizel briefly essays the high, heroic note, he comes off not much less shrill than Posthumus Leonatus. As a rule, though, the lovers in *WT* (who are not, after all, much more than teen-agers) are represented as good children finding refuge, by the favor of fortune and the flowering of their own natures, from the storm clouds of the world. Time as a hidden process is an ingredient in this development, as it is in all human affairs; but Time as a self-explanatory personage on a stage contributes to marking the character of the play as an idyll.

Nothing emerges more strikingly from a comparison of *Pandosto* with *WT* than the enormous expansion that Shakespeare constructed on the basis of half a sentence in Greene. "There was a meeting of all the farmers' daughters in Sicilia, whither Fawnia was also bidden as the mistress of the feast"; after the meeting is all over, and Fawnia is on her way home, Dorastus catches sight of her, and the story proceeds on its way. The sheep-shearing feast with all its appurtenances—the double appearance of Autolycus, the byplay with Mopsa and Dorcas, the dance of the "saltiers," the lurking presence of Polixenes and Camillo hovering suspiciously in the background, the probing questions, followed by the king's explosive reaction—all that is Shakespeare's addition. The material is particularly rich theatrically—not only the costumes of the shepherds, but the hairy extravagant dancers and their music, the several ballads and plentiful gewgaws of Autolycus the peddler, and the flowers of Perdita with her moralizing on them, make the scene immediately appealing. Like pastorals in general, the sheep-shearing scene appeals as both homely and exotic to an audience of urban theater-goers. For all that Shakespeare has taken pains to keep it from seeming too pretty, the material in a sense got the better of him. Historically, it has been hard for a director who had a seductive nymph to play Perdita to keep this

longest and most charming of her scenes from overbalancing
the rest of the play.

Nor, I think, should he try too hard. Perdita as Flora and
Florizel as her elected lover are to dominate the second half
of the play, and neither has had a chance to make any impression at all in the first three acts. She is a creature of the fields
and flowery meadows, as her predecessor Marina, of *Per.*,
was a creature of the salt sea. Discussing the four romances
synoptically as if they were parts of a single composition
encourages one to feel that dominant themes like the infant
caught in a storm at sea recur in all of them. But there is no
sign of such a theme in *Cym.*, and though the rudiments of
such a configuration can be found in *WT*, it is hard to feel
that it carries any such weight as can be placed on it in the
first and last of the romances.

For in *WT* the storm at sea occurs only after Antigonus
and Perdita have set foot on shore; its impact as a storm is
deliberately muted (as noted above) by the Clown's peculiar
idiom in describing it; and its practical function is simply to
destroy Antigonus (who thinks Perdita is really Polixenes'
child) before he can reach the king and give away the plot
to come. The storm is a danger, no doubt, of the sort through
which heroines and heroes of romance have been passing
since prehistory. But, compared with the materials Shakespeare immediately inherited, and on which he formed his
play, *WT* sharply reduces the pathos and the peril of the
storm-tossed babe. In Greene's novel, Perdita is cast adrift
alone in a skiff amid a mighty tempest that wafts her for-
tuitously to the seacoast of Bohemia. Either to make her trip
more credible or to give himself more room to introduce
Shepherd and Clown, Shakespeare made the voyage deliberate on the part of Antigonus and the storm an actual after-
math. The bear's removal of Antigonus was a narrative
necessity which distracted from the perils of Perdita; and a
second storm, threatening the lovers on their flight to Pan-

dosto's court, Shakespeare eliminated in a subordinate clause.

Thus the heroines of the four romances are better approached as a constellation of four individuals between whom mental lines can be drawn, than as a single entity four times treated with variations. Perdita and Marina, because they are both lost for some years in the middle of their plays, seem to be most closely akin. But their stories as well as the associations connected with them are quite different. The rebirth theme in WT applies to Hermione, not her daughter; like Imogen, Perdita is firmly attached to her lover, if not before the play starts, at any rate from the moment she becomes an adult in it; Marina is assigned to Lysimachus at the last minute. Perdita is by no means so firmly attached as Marina to the ideal of devotional chastity; her expectation, frankly stated, is to "breed" by young Florizel. More boldly though less directly marked out are differences in characterization deriving from WT's repeated, undisguised allusions to its own artifice.

This trait, recurrently noticeable in Shakespeare's earlier plays, is exceptionally prominent in WT. The play's very title announces it as a tale for long winter evenings—of no value, in other words, except to kill time—though indeed it might carry another overtone, to be conveyed in a subtitle: Waiting for Proserpina. Mamillius in II.1 promises to tell his mother a tale, and because a sad tale is best for winter, begins one about sprites and goblins, oblivious to the fact that the goblin who is his father is hovering over both their heads and about to pounce. The reconciliation of Act V is said to be "so like an old tale that the verity of it is in strong suspicion." These passing allusions in the text of the play to its own improbability or artifice are very different from the interventions of Gower in Per. After the first few lines of his introductory speech, Gower's comments are devoted mainly to forwarding the story. He is in service to it, particularly in moving the audience's imagination across great tracts of space and the time-span required for Marina to grow up. He commends the story with great seriousness, as one which is all the better for being old; instead of accentuating its improbabilities, he minimizes them. When the characters, speaking from inside WT, repeatedly emphasize the minimal grounds for accepting it, they issue in effect a challenge. Accepting the story, in spite of its own disclaimers, for what can be made of it, becomes a test to be passed:

> It is required [says Paulina]
> You do awake your faith.
>> (V.iii,94 f.)

That faith *quia absurdum* grows out of repeatedly insinuated doubts about the ground-bass illusions of narrative, which are sustained action, undistracted focus, and characters credible in themselves. The higher faith is required when the drama casts aside or directly mocks such tangible devices of persuasion. Instead of being invited or lured, one is provoked into belief. This may be one reason why, when the central characters of WT gather in the circle of *agape* at the play's end, they appear almost diaphanous in their fragility.

In diminishing WT as a stage action that can be followed with what Stendhal called *"femme de chambre"* absorption, I clearly mean to build higher. Verbally, it's the most rarefied of the romances in that its clowns, clods, dairymaids, and pickpockets speak the language of poetic invention no less than its kings and queens. Imaginatively, it allows and elicits flights. Perdita can be little more than a pert piece, or as paired with this figure or that, little less than a cosmic natural principle. The language is not always in service to character or plot; the play is full of vacant spaces and distances, across which language can and does reverberate. The cloud of disease that in Act I descends from nowhere on king Leontes is answered, not structurally but tonally, by the *Heilgesang* of Act IV (cf. Beethoven, Quartet #15). The death of Antigonus, shocking, comic, and abrupt, creates another sort of vacancy in the play's texture that is left raw and open till Paulina, late in the play, remembers. Non-motivations, some striking, some discreet, are frequent; scenes that an audience can anticipate being made are not. Polixenes' famous homily to Perdita that

> nature is made better by no mean
> But nature makes that mean—
>
> so that grafting
>
> Which does mend nature, change it rather, but
> The art itself is nature,
>
> (IV.iv.89 ff.)

—radiates in dozens of directions throughout the play—except on the man who speaks it. It encompasses the joining of Florizel to Perdita, plain shepherds enacting mythical parts, royal destinies interwoven with bumpkin accidents, the play itself as an artful construct celebrating natural impulses. These are remote allusions to be pursued by the individual fancy—intimations, not assertions. They may well be limitless. The unremarked name of Autolycus hangs out at a distance from the rest of the play; the seacoast of Bohemia is an ancient joke that at a stroke renders the play's geography pretend. Just when we have half-adjusted to Julio Romano as a time joke, his entire story explodes like a soap-bubble.

This sense of airy vacancy in the play contributes to a lack of moral pressure that may well be one of the most precious things about it. Though presented with exactly the opposite intent, allegorical teachings and ethical formulas imposed on the play diminish it even more radically than the genial, easy assumption that it's no more than a bit of verbal fluff. Without much mental strain—if one's willing to settle for a play on this level—one can take *WT* as the narrative of king Leontes, who sins deeply in Act I, and through a process of contrition, repentance, and the intervention of heavenly grace (represented at one's discretion by the Oracle, Hermione, Perdita, or Paulina who can carry an optional extra identity as Saint Paul) is restored to righteousness in Act V. Most of this story has to be understood as taking place off stage, and most of what does take place on stage in the middle acts is irrelevant to this story. The formula itself, looked at with a hard eye, is little more than the lowest common multiple of didactic narrative: an agent acts, errs, learns, is rewarded. But the lesson can be extracted, and indeed the same procedure can be repeated with Autolycus, who after sinning in Act III may be supposed to repent, reform, and display contrition in his conversation with Shepherd and Clown in Act V. There is no surer way to reduce a play to a glassy-eyed trophy head nailed to an academic wall.

Tonality in *WT* looms larger the more the play makes fun of its own narrative "truth"; conscious indirection, harmonic bridging, and mythical implications take on expressive as well as atmospheric functions behind the diminished action on the stage apron in which Prince Whatsisname wins the heart and hand of Princess Whoever. There is emphatically a visionary, though not a theological component in the play; it is diffused, not concentrated, and how much Christianity it contains depends mostly on how much you bring to it. The action takes place in a world beneficent and orderly on the whole. (Not invariably: the fate of Antigonus remains shocking because it is neither orderly, beneficent, nor explained.) The return of the two surly kings to mental health is accomplished, not by penitential discipline, least of all on the part of Polixenes, but by passage of time and processes of nature, with an assist from fortune. The climate of belief implied in the play is incurious and uncritical to a degree, but it fills the cosmos; the characters breathe the air of an unquestioning eclecticism, but it renders the commonplace luminous. At that concluding uncanonical ceremonial which brings the families together, we smile at the absurd neatness of it all, yet are touched by the thought of a new spring for the familiar world. Nature itself is a sacramental presence in the play; it is dirt, it is holy; given the blessing of art, it is all the more nature. By spelling out little but suggesting much, WT manages to be both a very simple play and one on which meditation can linger long and spread widely.

REFERENCES

Curious information about the history of Greene's *Pandosto*, especially its adventures in French translation, is provided by J. J. Jusserand in his introduction to WT for the Harper (Cambridge) edition of the *Complete Works*, gen. ed. Sidney Lee, Vol. VIII.

Nevill Coghill in a sharp, cogent contribution titled "Six Points of Stage-Craft in the Winter's Tale" (*Shakespeare Survey* 11, 1958) directly attacks the presumption that it is an ill-made play.

S. L. Bethell in *The Winter's Tale* (Staples Press, New York and London, N.D.) imposes on the play or derives from it a Christian interpretation which will appeal to some readers as parochial.

J. A. Bryant, Jr., writing on "Shakespeare's Allegory" in *Sewanee Review* LXIII (1955), achieves an extreme in the literal-minded and heavy-handed interpretation of the play.

F. D. Hoeniger, "The Meaning of the Winter's Tale" in *The University of Toronto Quarterly* XX, 1 (October, 1950), is more temperate and tactful in proposing his allegories than either of the above.

The Proserpina-Demeter parallel was first suggested in 1884 by W. F. C. Wigston, *A New Study of Shakespeare*—a book not to be found in many of the respectable bibliographies because by a Baconian. Before applying to *WT* the word "myth" or the adjective "mythical" in any sense more expansive than that of an allusion to classical mythology, one should consult the dry, analytic article of Wallace W. Douglas, "The Meanings of 'Myth' in Modern Criticism," in *MP* 50 (1952–53), p. 235.

V

THE TEMPEST

THREE FACTS ABOUT *Tmp.*—ALL TRUE, ALL OF QUESTIONABLE import—frame any discussion of the drama. It was Shakespeare's last complete play, if not the last work he did for the theater; unusually among the dramas, it occupies restricted space and limited time, that is, observes the "unities"; and though there are some sources and many analogues for particular details of scene, action, or verbal expression, no single source provided the armature for *Tmp.*—as the core of *Per.* derives from the legend of Apollonius, the main component of *Cym.* from *Decameron* II.9, and most of *WT* from *Pandosto*. All three of these facts can be made to point toward a single conclusion, that Shakespeare worked on *Tmp.* with particular care—hence that if he cherished an allegorical (but more properly a metaphorical) message to be delivered to the world, he probably delivered it here. The play has been so often approached from this point of view that a commentator writing in the late 20th century might well—if only to make the ulterior meaning work for a living—look around for another approach. And in fact there are some indicators that point in quite the contrary direction. *Tmp.* makes use of an exotic setting, non-human or quasi-human characters, spectacles, and considerable music, all of which divert the eye and ear without necessarily giving the analytic mind much to linger on. The major plot elements, such as a rightful ruler and a usurping brother, a lost princess discovered by her susceptible prince, were long-familiar ingredients of Shakespeare's narrative practice. Not exactly in opposition to the first view of the play, this second set of qualities implies that the poet may have been more concerned to evoke feelings and moods than to express a direct set of correspondences. Metaphor and allegory depend on a second level of reference that can be reached from the first and related to it. Perhaps the deeper meanings being sought in *Tmp.* are phantoms rising from the practice of demanding more certainties than the poet was ever of a mind to deliver. Though applicable to all the romances, this dilemma has attached itself with particular tenacity over the 19th and 20th centuries to *Tmp.*

To start far back with some details of production and publication, the first staging of *Tmp.* about which we know, though probably not the first that ever took place, occurred on Hallowmass night (November 1) of 1611 at Whitehall. The text cannot well have been written after that; and the date before which it cannot have been written, though not so precise, is also clearly defined. The play incorporates material from William Strachey's account of the wreck of the *Sea-Adventure* on the islands of Bermuda, in 1609. Strachey's pamphlet did not appear till 1610; Shakespeare's play is thus dated within a period of less than two years. It is not often that we can assign such precise dates to a play of that age; there is accordingly no reason to strain after greater particularity. After its first performance or performances, *Tmp.* had a second and particularly glamorous production. During the winter of 1612–13, as part of those court ceremonials honoring the betrothal and marriage of Princess Elizabeth—at

which *WT* was presented—Shakespeare's troupe was also
called on to produce, amid the clatter and clutter of a royal
occasion, *Tmp*. It could have been performed for either betrothal or marriage festivities, and the text could have been
altered for the occasion, most likely in connection with the
masque of Ceres, Juno, and Iris. But this guess leaves several
loose ends; without a masque in Act IV, the 1611 version of
the play must have been strangely truncated, and if the
masque when added did refer to dynastic events, breaking
it off with rough horseplay like the hunting down of Caliban
and his cronies does not seem like a suave gesture for concluding a royal compliment. Whatever the ways in which
the play was adapted to its several occasions and possible
venues (and obviously they are hard to know in any detail
and with any assurance), the text of the play as it exists for
us derives from a single source, the First Folio of 1623, where
it takes pride of place. Perhaps because of its prominence,
Tmp. was carefully prepared for the printer. The text is divided into acts and scenes, the punctuation is both correct
and consistent, a *dramatis personae* is prefixed. Here, as often
elsewhere in Shakespeare, lineation is sometimes a problem;
whether Caliban speaks verse, prose, or something in between, may provide questions; but generally the text is clear.

Under the head of borrowing trouble, theories of an earlier
version, whether written by Shakespeare in his youth or by
someone else, can without rashness be disregarded. Though
this sort of thing is always possible, simply because of the
difficulty of proving a negative, the chronology of composition largely precludes it here. As for the somewhat more
substantial matter of what parts of Shakespeare's reading
entered into the play's making, it may be useful to set out
the various possibilities in rough order of their likelihood.

1. Montaigne's essay "On Cannibals," written around
   1580 and translated by Florio in 1603, could have been

known to Shakespeare in either French or English; it definitely underlies Gonzalo's musings in Act II on the primitive life.

2. A set of three pamphlets describing a shipwreck on the Bermudas and the founding of an English colony in Virginia appeared in 1610; the most likely of these to have influenced Shakespeare's play is the narrative of William Strachey which describes a fierce storm and shipwreck. Since the days of Columbus and Vespucci travellers to the New World had been accumulating descriptions both of the country and its inhabitants. Occasionally we can find a specific source for a specific detail; "Setebos" is mentioned as a Patagonian god in Robert Eden's *History of Travaile* (1577), and in a general way it seems likely that Shakespeare had read widely in the literature of exploration.

3. Italian narrative materials about dynastic feuds and domestic jealousies could have reached Shakespeare through collections of *novelle*, prose or verse romances, and formal histories. Several play-outlines (*scenari*) from the *commedia dell' arte* include narrative units like those in *Tmp.*; though not fully written out in the manner of a play-script, they could have reached Shakespeare by way of troupes of Italian comedians who visited London and performed there.

4. Classical lore, as in Ovid, Virgil, Longus, Heliodorus, Apollonius Rhodius, the pastoral poets, and the mythographers, entered into Shakespeare's background either directly or through the work of Italian or English imitators. The English masque (as in the work of Jonson), the English romance (as in the work of Sidney), and the English romance-epic (as in the work of Spenser) cannot but have had an influence on Shakespeare, though it is only here and there that we can lay our

finger on a bit of persuasive evidence for a specific influence.

5. The wide field of international folklore provides many partial parallels for many isolated units of *Tmp.*'s narrative. One can trace across the centuries and continents themes such as the shipwreck, the magician, the wild man, the lost princess, the jealous brother, the puck or will-o'-the-wisp, not to mention such immemorial actions as forgiveness of enemies, pairing off of true lovers, restoring of order, and expulsion of black villainy. These are, so to speak, the plankton and foraminifera of Europe's narrative waters; no bay, no inlet is without them, no imagination can avoid ingesting them.

Most of the evidence that Shakespeare drew on any part of this material for the composition of *Tmp.* consists of parallel passages, more or less close, extended, and distinctive. A name like "Setebos," which is odd, and occurs in only one possible source, determines Shakespeare's use of that source; storms at sea, of which there are thousands in the literature, generally carry with them an array of similar if not identical properties, half a dozen of which in Shakespeare's play do nothing to establish that he drew on one source rather than another. Even when he took from a useful predecessor, he had no hesitation about adapting and eliminating or adding to suit his purposes. Of the three "Bermuda" pamphlets, it seems clear he relied most heavily on Strachey's *True Reportory.* The storm and shipwreck provided strong and stirring material, of which Shakespeare took such advantage as his stage-medium would allow; but the island on which the *Sea Adventure*'s people straggled ashore was uninhabited, and Shakespeare populated it with creatures from his reading and his imagination. He quietly half-transferred it from the Atlantic or Caribbean to the Mediterranean without disturbing its exotic tropical foliage or its most primitive inhabitant, a kind of semi-human Indian whose mother may have been a witch from Algiers. In a word, whatever his sources, Shakespeare dealt freely with them, more freely even than he had done with his sources in many earlier plays.

One major architectural feature of *Tmp.* is the introduction of a miniature court-society, stratified into classes and divided by jealousies and old intrigues, into a new environment where the truth about itself is in various ways revealed. A particularly telling if unobtrusive indicator about the royal party wrecked on Prospero's island concerns the recent wedding of Alonso's daughter Claribel to the king of Tunis. Speaking to the despondent Alonso, Sebastian makes (II.i) the sharp but uncontradicted point that the troubles of the king of Naples are of his own making, since Claribel herself was "loath" to marry the monarch of Tunis, and did so only out of obedience to her father. As we never see Claribel or hear any more about her, the fact that she was pushed into an unwelcome marriage doesn't much strike us (slothful, unimaginative audience that we are); but as a piece of gratuitous invention, it stands out. To say nothing about her feelings would have been easy; we should have assumed that she was a joyful or at least a contented bride. To the plot's motion it would make no difference at all. But dynastic marriages, like conspiratorial rivals conniving after supreme power, were frequent if unlovely marks of "civilized" European society. The collusion of Alonso and Antonio against Prospero, followed by the plot of Antonio and Sebastian against Alonso, and parodied by the conspiracy of Caliban and his cronies against Prospero—these repeated festerings in the body politic give us a sour image of the civilized social order. And meanwhile Claribel cries her eyes out in distant Tunis—not merely in another kingdom but on another continent and with strong implications of an alien culture and an unfamiliar religion. It is interesting, and not uncharacter-

istic of the romances, that the few sharp, dry words devoted
to her fate come from the mouth of Sebastian, her uncle. He
is by no means a sentimentalist—something of a villain,
rather, though scarcely a strong one. One needn't suppose
his words of reproach to Alonso are inspired by any particular tenderness for Claribel. They may, in keeping with his
acerb, sardonic character, be a kind of conscious therapy for
distracting the king from his grief—serving the same end,
though with more energy, that Gonzalo attempts with his
platitudes. Or one may read behind them a purpose of the
playwright's, to make evident the harshness of social custom
and parental authority, among the "civilized."

This contrast between civilization and nature, frequently
to the detriment of the former, comes as no surprise, surely;
but it's neither one-sided nor oppressive, rather it forms part
of the framework-background for the action. And that action
involves neither abstractions, attitudes, nor symbols, but
characters on a stage. First and foremost of these is Prospero,
the supplanted duke of Milan, the wizard who raised the
originating storm, the protector and bestower of Miranda,
and in short the contriver and controller of the play's action.
As a legitimate ruler plotted against by an ambitious usurping
brother, Prospero brings into *Tmp.* a long Shakespearean
lineage and a record of unbroken sympathy. A close parallel
is with *As You Like It*, where Duke Senior has been exiled to
the Forest of Arden by his brother Frederick—a schemer
whose cruel designs are diverted only at the last minute (and
most improbably) by an accidental encounter with "an old
religious man." The elder Hamlet is another legitimate monarch destroyed by the malicious machinations of an unscrupulous usurper, his brother. The uneasy relation between
Don Pedro and Don John of *Much Ado* provides another
parallel; still another, less pressing, could be found in the
antithesis between Duncan the legitimate monarch and Macbeth the underhanded pretender. After Bolingbroke's au-

dacious act in unkinging Richard II, the stain of his son's hereditary guilt lingers on even amid all the patriotic clatter of *Henry V*. Shakespeare consistently assumes a legitimist position in these matters; and so he does in *Tmp*. We hear the story of the coup by which Prospero was deposed only from the mouth of the aggrieved victim; the crime is aggravated because brother is betraying brother; and when Antonio discusses the matter with Sebastian, he dismisses mention of his conscience with a villain's callous carelessness:

> if 'twere a kibe,
> 'Twould put me to my slipper: but I feel not
> This deity in my bosom.
>
> (II.i.270 ff.)

To have Prospero and his daughter exiled on a desert island while a double-eyed blackguard like Antonio rules over Milan and swims in the favor of the king of Naples amounts to a major cosmic unbalance. The prime work of the play will be to correct it. Prospero is not only the main victim of this injustice but the agent whose special powers act to restore the natural and correct state of things.

I labor thus to establish (what the common reader sensibly takes for granted) the centrality of Prospero and his story, because it's also possible to see the adventures of the royal party on the island as a testing and illuminating experience equivalent in some ways to the ancient mysteries. This is an appealing prospect for the interpreter, because it seems to direct the play toward a region of religious awe which presumably heightens (or deepens) its significance. The point is not one to be dismissed out of hand, though Shakespeare has scattered some deliberate difficulties across its path; but, even given all the weight it can possibly support, the story of Alonso/Antonio's illumination must take its place within the larger vault of Prospero's rarer action.

The basis for that action is laid out for the audience, with less art than Shakespeare usually invokes, in the long monologue of Prospero, with brief interruptions by Miranda, that occupies the first part of scene ii, Act I. We need say the less about it because no part of it comes into later question, and most of it is simply assumed as a basis for further action. Between his own scholarly absent-mindedness or loose good nature, and the crass duplicity of his brother, Prospero, it appears, was deprived of his dignity and power. Anxious scanners of the far horizon have sometimes worried whether, after his return from the island and with his magical powers abjured, he will be able to provide Milan with effectual rule. But Shakespeare has guarded against his appearing to be an amiable dotard by giving him an imperious temper and strict control over Ferdinand, Caliban, and the royal party as a whole. In many stories about magicians and wizards, including some of the Italian *scenari*, the mage displays an uncertain temper and a penchant for playing tricks or imposing tasks on lesser mortals. Perhaps Shakespeare welcomed such a predisposition as a useful *trouvaille*; perhaps, bearing in mind Prospero's previous experiences, he made him crusty in consequence. Whether he made his wizard too severe in his relations with Ariel and (especially) Caliban is a later question. Certainly he went out of his way to have Prospero emphasize "the love my people bore me" and the indignities inflicted on Milan by Antonio's rule, so we should be confident of his welcome return. And in dealing with the intruders on his island—whether hostile, friendly, or just puzzled—Shakespeare carefully shows Prospero exercising what his age would have called "statecraft." From our perspective, it may appear more natural to call it "stagecraft."

Whatever his capacity, Prospero disposes of his guest/prisoners briskly and efficiently. Most of the ship's crew, who would be cumbersome by their very numbers, are stowed aboard the vessel under hatches, and put quietly to sleep.

(A lot of miscellaneous sleeping takes place in this play: it contributes to the languid, unreal atmosphere of the island, and it may serve—witness the inconvenient crew—as a temporary storage device. Whether it is anything more is arguable. No sleeper except Caliban remembers the content of his dreams, and Caliban's dreams are outside the time-frame of the play.) The other intruders are separated into three groups: Ferdinand, the court-party, and that precious pair Stephano and Trinculo. Consistently kept apart from one another, their stories are intertwined according to a not very elaborate pattern:

I.ii.375 to end of act	Ferdinand
II.i.	Court party (assassination plot)
ii. to end of act	Stephano, Trinculo
III.i	Ferdinand
ii	Stephano, Trinculo
iii	Court party (banquet)
IV.i to 165	Ferdinand (masque)
i.195 to end of act	Stephano, Trinculo
V.	Court party + Ferdinand, Miranda + crew + Stephano, Trinculo

From the moment he lays eyes on Miranda, Ferdinand needs relatively little control, and the penance Prospero imposes on him, explained from the beginning as a kind of mock-testing, is easily performed; the handsome young actor to whom the part falls need not fear getting his jerkin dirty or his hands scratched. The royal party, as a more complex social group, calls for more devious management. They are, when first placed on stage, exhausted by their misadventures at sea, bewildered by the island, and dispirited by the loss of prince Ferdinand. They are also helpless in the absence of experienced sailors and knowledgeable workmen.* This point is not made in the text, perhaps because it could be made by costuming. The court costumes of the royal party— unsoiled, unstained, holding their freshness and glosses— can only contribute to a sense of comic inappropriateness in a tropical rain forest. In addition to their practical helplessness, expressed not simply in their doing nothing, but in their having no idea of what to do, the castaways are riven by factional antipathies. At first these take the form of continual sneers directed by Antonio and Sebastian at old Gonzalo; but as soon as a carefully selective charm has laid the rest of the party to sleep, Antonio begins egging Sebastian into a plot to murder Alonso and Gonzalo. Lurking invisibly in the neighborhood, Ariel overhears the plot, and without making his presence known, frustrates it; he also, as we are to understand, reports it to Prospero.

The forces here revealed could easily, if given a little more or a little different emphasis, develop very somber overtones. What Prospero does with his secret knowledge could mean a quick and disagreeable end for both conspirators. (It is not, I think, extraneous to recall what happens to Cambridge, Grey, and Scroop in the second act of *Henry V*; if Prospero at any time tells Alonso what he knows, the two conspirators will get equally short shrift.) Dramatically as well, the plot against Alonso is strong stuff; it is fratricide added to regicide that the royal party brings to the island; and though their scheme is put off for the moment in II.i, a few lines in III.iii remind the audience, if nobody else, that it is only on hold.

---

* Strachey's report emphatically remarked that the Bermuda castaways on reaching Virginia did not even know how to catch fish in adequate quantities; in Bermuda, on the other hand, they had found wild hogs in plenty, tortoises, and birds of whose innocence it was easy to take advantage. Shakespeare, however, having only a sojourn of a couple of hours to account for, could be relatively casual about food supplies; Stephano and Trinculo, the "low" characters, are the only ones concerned with food— and, of course, drink.

Obviously a comedy cannot contain very much of a conspiracy as dark and bloody as that of Macbeth and his wife
against Duncan; and Shakespeare has attenuated it. Prospero
leaves his knowledge of the plot in abeyance till Act V, and
then he very discreetly only half-solves the problem. In what
must be an aside (though V.126 was only so labelled in
Johnson's edition of 1765), he lets slip his knowledge to
Antonio and Sebastian, leaving a threat to tell all hanging
over them. For purposes of the play, this suffices admirably.
At the moment when Ferdinand and Miranda are being
united in holy matrimony, nobody wants to see the play's
villains haled before the bar of justice and decapitated. King
Alonso, to be sure, is left with a secret viper in his court;
we assume that Prospero will keep a wary eye on Antonio,
but Sebastian is still unexposed and presumably dangerous.
On the other hand, he is the lesser of the two villains, and
the king of Naples probably deserves nothing more from
Prospero than he gets. In this rough and ready, but actually
rather artful way, Prospero takes command of the most serious political complication of the drama; it doesn't appear
that we have to worry about his capacity to rule Milan when
he gets there.*

Prospero's second major encounter with the royal party is
the banquet scene (or, as it really should be called, the
denunciation-scene) of III.iii. An illusory banquet, summoned up by spirits, is snatched away by them before anyone can taste it. Apart from providing visual window-
dressing, the pattern of this action conforms with a consistent
strain in Prospero's handling of the castaways, i.e., it is an
act of tantalizing. The special form of the story involving

---

* How Prospero's pledge to "tell no tales" (129) agrees with the phrase
"would here have killed your king" (78) I cannot explain. One can only
guess that Alonso, who has entered "with a frantic gesture," does not
hear or understand the first speech. But that is not exactly Prospero's
doing. To go by the script, he has already told the worst tale he knows.

harpies and a banquet dates back to the *Argonautica* of Apollonius, where the victim is Phineus; but Shakespeare doubtless had in mind the later Virgilian version, where Aeneas and his fellow-adventurers are first enticed with viands, then rebuffed by the savage, squalid birds. In addition, Celaeno, the chief harpy, delivers a dire prophecy to the Trojans, warning them of desperate hardships before they reach their goal. Ariel, when he puts on the semblance of a harpy and delivers a fierce denunciation of Prospero's enemies, assumes not only the prophetic status of Celaeno but an identification with the winds, of which harpies are traditional emblems. One of their frequent functions is to carry off guilty humans direct to the underworld; thus both nature and the diabolically unnatural seem united to drive the men of sin out of their wits and into headlong flight. But in fact the *Aeneid*-parallel can be stretched only so far. The royal party includes no epic hero on an epic mission; Ariel as mock-harpy makes no prophecy about the future, only discloses a past crime. Though superficial appearances make against it, the stronger parallel is with *Hamlet*'s Mousetrap, as a brief pageant eliciting from specific spectators an open expression of hitherto hidden guilt.

As he will later hunt with dogs Caliban, Stephano, and Trinculo, so Prospero herds the royal party into a circle near his cave, and freezes them there, spiritually as well as physically. Though they are, in the wizard's phrase, "all knit up," distinctions are made: the king is inwardly thunderstruck, Antonio and Sebastian sit sullen and still, Gonzalo weeps. The display—executed by Ariel, orchestrated by Prospero— has attained its proper, proportional effects, and the party can be put on hold till the resolutions and explanations of Act V. Whether Gonzalo has actually heard the admonition is moot. He has certainly seen the banquet and the harpy, and it would be hard for an audience to suppose that he did not hear what was loud and clear to them. But the message has no direct effect on him; he knows who the three "men of sin" are, and that he is not one of them. For the moment, he must submit to being marshalled into the magic circle with the rest of the courtiers.

Caliban and his semi-civilized soul-mates Stephano and Trinculo provide Prospero with another set of much easier tests. Whether one considers him a Caribbean cannibal or a bastard son of the devil by an Algerian witch named Sycorax,* Caliban clearly can claim the island by direct descent from its first inhabitant: before Sycorax, it was unpeopled. It's with some reason, then, that he complains of Prospero as a usurper and a tyrant who, having coaxed and wheedled him into revealing the secrets of the island, has enslaved him and held him to servile tasks. The impression is as disagreeable as if a rigorous legal official should sentence Falstaff to the workhouse. Caliban is unlovely but fascinating on the stage, not only by virtue of his novelty, but because of his amorphous, unashamed libido. Like Cloten, he is all gut and brag—cowardly yet swaggering, bibulous and timorous, lustful and impulsive, stinking and unashamed. And most wonderfully of all, deep within him, as within Cloten, lurks a streak of poetry.

To a large extent and for a long time, Prospero doesn't have to do anything *against* Caliban, because he degrades, exposes, and ridicules himself. Amid the mutual abuse and recriminations of I.ii, one thing comes clear, that he tried to rape Miranda, feels no shame over it, and still hopes to do it if he can. That takes him, once and for all, outside our

---

* Many speculations surround the name of Caliban's mother, but the upshot is that out of numerous possibilities, no particular source can be conclusively assigned. Analogues with Circe—a goddess on an island consorting with heroes—don't readily agree with her being a pregnant witch in Algiers, which since the mid-16th century had been a seat of the Barbary pirates. If anything, the mythology mitigates and ennobles what we are given as fact.

sympathies. His cowering before the thunder is of a piece with his slavish servility before Stephano and Trinculo, whom in an ecstasy of self-abasement he proclaims not just his masters but his gods. His helpless susceptibility to strong drink completes the picture; it may be anthropologically correct, but it destroys whatever original sympathy an audience had with Caliban as a noble native destroyed by predatory colonialists.

By rights, Stephano and Trinculo ought to be sleeping under hatches with the rest of the ship's crew; Shakespeare has let them out, partly for comic effect, partly in compliance with the Bermuda-pamphlets story, to illustrate the dangerous folly of irresponsible mutiny. Like Jack Cade and his men in *Henry VI, Part 2*, but here in alliance with the primitive Caliban, they want to destroy all order and degree, live without labor, and escape the tyranny of book-learning. In one direction, they provide a parodic counter to Gonzalo's naive musings about the idyllic state of nature; at another level, they provide a degrading commentary on the conspiratorial courtiers, who are equally impatient under the constraints of lawful authority. And here particularly the deepening violence of Caliban's fantasies recalls those of Cloten. After capturing Prospero in his sleep,

> there thou mayst brain him,
> Having first seiz'd his books; or with a log
> Batter his skull, or paunch him with a stake,
> Or cut his wezand with thy knife;
>
> (III.ii.86 ff.)

they will then share out Miranda and live like kings on the isle.

Since all this plotting is done in secret, and while the conspirators are increasingly drunk, there is nothing that Prospero and his agents need do, beyond having Ariel keep an eye on them; his teasing of them, from the vantage of his invisibility, is his own private joke, and has no consequences. Indeed, one major implication of their plotting reflects inward; they endanger outward authority less than they reveal the anarchy of their own spirits. Like Cloten again, they indulge a riot of chaotic, incompatible appetites; and in this respect they contrast sharply with the mutineers of Strachey's Bermuda narrative, who were for the most part puritans and men of an uncommonly pious disposition. The change adds emphasis, if emphasis were needed, to a psychological reading of *Tmp.*'s vulgar rebellion.

In fact, Prospero doesn't have to take action against the trio of knaves till the end of Act IV, and then simply by catching them in a trap so elementary that even Caliban can recognize it, a display of gaudy garments: "let it alone, thou fool; it is but trash," he tells his erstwhile "god." The glittering costumes hung out to catch shallow fools could doubtless be moralized into a reproof of those who prize show over substance, etc., but the point needn't be labored. As for the subsequent pursuit by dogs, though foxhunting has become since the 18th century an exclusive pursuit of the gentry, that shouldn't obscure the fact that in Shakespeare's day any sort of vermin could be pursued with a pack. The tumultuous chase, coming directly after the stately, slow-paced masque, has prompted thoughts of the hunt as an anti-masque. But this is a short-sighted and much too literary fancy. The low conspirators have been permitted to cultivate their crude fantasies in relative immunity; they must now be punished and humiliated, as their "betters" have been punished and humiliated before them, if the action is to maintain its balance. In the end, it's worth noting, Caliban gets his freedom on the same terms as Ariel gets his; he will not have to haul any more logs, his birthright will be restored to him; yet it's impressive how little joy the prospect seems to give him. Will he hear music and dream dreams when he is alone

on the island? Every reader must answer to his own imaginings, but one is permitted to hope.

It has been easy and natural to talk about Prospero as a
political man with only passing reference to his skills as a
magician. In fact, his art, as made visually evident in his
robe, can be put on and off at pleasure. It gives him command
of an impressive range of powers. Ariel can, in his traditional
role as familiar spirit, be summoned and dispatched in an
instant; he can be made visible or invisible as occasion requires. Apart from Ariel, an indefinite number of other spirits
serve at Prospero's beck, watching over Caliban and plaguing
him with pinches and agues as requested. The wizard can
recognize an approaching ship and identify its passengers at
a great distance, can raise storms and allay them, can create
apparitions like the banquet and the masque then instantly
vaporize them, can immobilize those who oppose him or
make them sleep when he chooses. "Thy nerves are in their
infancy again," he tells Ferdinand, and immediately they are.
Because his supernatural skills are clearly different from those
of Sycorax, we are invited to suppose that they are derived
from a different source, are theurgic rather than goetic, in
other words white rather than black magic. But in fact Shakespeare not only avoids but muddles the question of where
they come from. Sycorax, in the long tradition of witches
stretching from Theocritus, is associated with the moon
(V.269), hence with Hecate, goddess of witchcraft; but there
is no contrasting planet or deity for Prospero. His "books"
are very important to his powers, but what sort of books
they are we have no way of guessing; he is accompanied by
familiar spirits (Ariel is one of them), but they are neither
demons nor angels—indeterminate creatures, rather, half-
body, half-spirit—intelligences, geniuses, attendants. Prospero uses a very minimum of magical apparatus—no learned
incantations, occult names, or mysterious charms, such as
enliven *Friar Bacon and Friar Bungay*; at most he draws an

occasional circle with his wand, or makes a pass in the air. For his harmless horseplay with Caliban and his friends (III.ii) Ariel is not above borrowing some of Faustus' harmless horseplay in the papal court (also III.ii of Marlowe's play). No doubt in the course of performance the actor playing Prospero improvises gestures, signs, and symbols; but the more mysterious and impressive they are, the more ambiguous is likely to remain the source of their apparent extraordinary power. Ambiguity, it seems to me, is just the effect at which Shakespeare is aiming. Prospero has powers that neither immense natural wisdom nor profound supernatural devotion could give; he shows no great measure of either, least of all of the latter; thus his powers, though used for good, seem to be dangerous in their operation and obscure in their source. And this is one reason why, when the extraordinary perils of the plot have been averted, an audience is just the least bit relieved to find the mage breaking his staff and drowning his books.

Prospero, it will be remarked, has two speeches toward the end of *Tmp.* in which he bids farewell to his art. After breaking off the dance of nymphs and harvesters in IV.i, he addresses Ferdinand with the "Our revels now are ended" speech; then in V, just before releasing the prisoners from their enchantment, he speaks the "Ye elves of hills, brooks, standing lakes, and groves" speech. As poetry, they need no praise, but in terms of the occasion giving rise to them, both have been remarked as a little excessive, or at the least, off-key. The thought of "that foul conspiracy" angers Prospero into breaking off the masque abruptly; both Miranda and Ferdinand remark on his disturbed expression, and as soon as he can he turns to plan with Ariel his countermeasures. Yet in the meantime he answers for Ferdinand, in serene and flowing verse, a set of questions that have never been asked, about the nature of the masque, the masquers, of dramatic illusion itself, and about the permanence of the great globe and the human race. His answers imply questions infinite in both time and space; and the word "globe" as spoken on Shakespeare's stage had an inherent double allusion which could not help turning the audience's thinking back on itself and its present situation. The dissolution that Prospero summons up in this evocation of far-reaching illusionistic recollections extends far beyond anything that Ferdinand and Miranda, as spectators of the masque, have seen or been asked to imagine.

> The cloud-capp'd towers, the gorgeous palaces,
> The solemn temples,
>
> (IV.i.152–3)

the world and all its generations to come, but also "The Tempest" and its audience within their wooden O, enter into the play in the act of fading out of it. In the phrase, "we are such stuff / As dreams are made on," the infinite inclusiveness of "we" is matched by the infinite regress of dreams and dreamers, as if each individual viewer were invited to sink through layer after layer of himself, like Thaisa through the humming water of ocean.

Like the first, Prospero's second valedictory ("Ye elves of hills," etc.: V) puts before the audience a vivid awareness of the wizard's magical powers, even in the process of dismissing them. It is a more solemn and formal invocation, for which Shakespeare did not hesitate to coopt the majestic verses of Ovid's *Metamorphoses* (VII.197; Golding's translation, VII.265), in which Medea invokes the unearthly powers of Hecate. That Prospero in the very act of abjuring his magic comes so close to identifying it with that of the arch-witch (and so of Caliban's mother) openly confirms that ambiguity which earlier seemed to be just implied. In fact, the operation that Medea contemplates when she speaks her invocation is beneficent. She is about to restore old Aeson, Jason's father, to his virile youth. But to do so, she gathers such horrific properties, invokes such terrible powers, concocts such grotesque mixtures, that it's almost a relief when she slits the old man's throat and pours her foaming brew into his veins. In translating from Ovid's Latin, Shakespeare softened the details considerably; at the same time, he kept close enough to Golding's popular version so common readers would not have been hard pressed to catch the allusion. This formal abjuration, like the earlier dismissal of illusions, calls on the audience to imagine things it has not seen in the play. Particularly the boast that

> graves at my command
> Have wak'd their sleepers, op'd, and let 'em forth
> By my so potent Art,
>
> (V.48 ff.)

seems incompatible with Prospero's solitude on the island. But on a narrative level, the permanent abjuration of his art with its limitless powers marks another strong termination of the story.

Stasis is the primary effect sought by the ending of *Tmp.*, and it is achieved several times over, by Prospero's dissolution and abjuration speeches, by the masque itself with its implication that Miranda and Ferdinand are natural as well as political monarchs, by the revelation of the lovers playing chess, and finally by the forming of a human ring wider and warmer than any magician's compulsory circle. Shakespeare, who wrote no formal masques himself but watched the flowering of the form under Jonson's hands, cannot have been unaware of its capacity for bringing action to a motionless point. The idea of staging a private masque on a desert island for a couple of young innocents must have tickled both his sense of humor and his wish to end the play with a spectacle. Juno, Ceres, and Iris (three female deities promising domestic bliss, fecundity, and peace) vouch for the future of the marriage, the past having been brutally disfigured by jealous, competitive males. For the third time within a couple of minutes (cf. IV.i.13 and 50) they reiterate warnings against premature erotic indulgence, then introduce the cool nymphs and sunburnt sicklemen whose dance figures the tempered natural harmonies of happy marriage. Since the common ending of a masque (the performers mingling in dance with the audience) cannot well take place here, the vision breaks off with Prospero turning his attention to Caliban's plot, and the lovers put on hold in his cell.

The game of chess at which the lovers are discovered when they reappear (V.170) serves positive and negative ends. To the extent that Virgil's *Aeneid* lies latent behind the play, a pair of ardent new lovers hidden in a cave might suggest the fatal error of Dido and Aeneas; even without Virgil, the time passed by Ferdinand and Miranda away from Prospero's vigilant eyes and those of the suspicious audience, has to be accounted for by some innocent activity. Chess was a polite, an upper-class game, supposedly too intellectual for the lower orders; it is also a game of strategy, for training the wits of social leaders. Miranda's adapting to it instantly is evidence of her noble instincts and inherently spiritual nature. As mimic warfare, chess also suggests a symbolic resolution of those dynastic conflicts (Milan/Naples but by extension the notoriously entangled city-states of Italy) that had troubled the past. And it brings the play to a stop in yet another way by intimating withdrawal from the heat of action, existence on a cool, geometrical, two-dimensional plane.

The scheme sketched above (p. 132) for dividing the action stresses the way in which the last act adds one group of characters after another, including the crew members asleep under hatches, about whom a properly concerned audience will long since have forgotten. Their return brings the play back to its start, completing a stage-cycle just as assembling the entire cast of characters completes the narrative cycle. Prospero now has his dukedom, Miranda her prince (like previous occupants of that role, he is a bit of a tailor's dummy), Caliban his island, and Gonzalo his old tired joke about the boatswain's hanging face. All the plots have been foiled, though nobody has been excessively punished, or will be. The vessel and crew are restored as promised, and the adventure on the island is about to disappear into the past like a dream. It has not actually been a dream, more than any imaginary enclosed stage action resembles a dream; yet the characters repeatedly ask themselves whether they are awake or asleep, and the audience must similarly ask itself whether the coherent yet unreal atmosphere of the play—its *mood*—isn't, precisely, dreamlike.

Mood rather than action is the keynote to the final scene; it could be described as a strong sense of festive joy rising, perhaps, from a sense of sudden discovery. Miranda, who is herself a wonder, gives expression to it in her famous cry:

> O wonder!
> How many goodly creatures are there here!
> How beauteous mankind is! O brave new world,
> That has such people in it!
>
> (V.181 ff.)

She is talking, of course, about the characters on stage, and Prospero knows very well that her fine enthusiasm will soon fade into the dull drab of everyday. " 'Tis new to thee," he says, not sourly, but briefly and perhaps more as explanation to the others than as admonition to his daughter. Yet the fact is that her admiration includes not only everyone on stage—Sebastian who has recognized a miracle as well as sullen Antonio, who has not—but spills over onto the audience. Through the entire course of this play, and of almost all other plays, for that matter, the audience has tacitly defined itself as the quotidian, the commonplace deadweight viewer looking in on an exotic, quicksilver world. Here for a magic second the world looks back and finds us to be, not dull or repugnant, but wonderful—sort of, for the moment. It is a unique theatrical effect (to say no more); and though a few last strings remain to be tied, this instant fills the play to overflowing.

Where mood makes so much of the play, background emphases call for particular attention. The storm at sea, pretty surely drawing on Strachey's terrifying account in his *True Reportory*, makes its impression in the first act; and though no such overwhelming visions of ocean recur in the rest of the play, the sea is never far removed from action of imagery. Ariel's song to Ferdinand,

> Nothing of him that doth fade
> But doth suffer a sea-change
> Into something rich and strange
> (I.ii.402 ff.)

—though in fact it is only a malicious Puckish misleading, Alonso being dry and well—actually reverberates far beyond the immediate situation. Drowning is only the most radical of many sea-changes, and from beginning to end the play's action can be thought of as a series of such mutations. Old Gonzalo, sensible for once and even touched with the glowing coal of poetry, says as much in one of his last speeches (V.205); and though he attributes everything to those unfailing harbingers, "the gods," nature herself has acted, in the body of the play, as Destiny's agent. In his harpy-speech of denunciation, Ariel says it; "the powers" have

Incens'd the seas and shores, yea, all the creatures
Against your peace,

(III.iii.74 f.)

and Alonso believes it; he has heard the billows and the
thunder (III.iii.98) pronounce against his guilt. Among other
allied capacities, Ariel has served in the play as St. Elmo's
fire, a particularly nautical phenomenon; and though Caliban
was doubtless costumed on the Globe's stage like a regular
"salvage" man—shaggy, with long nails, big teeth, and a
rough fur cloak—he is repeatedly described as looking and
smelling like a fish.* At the play's end, Sebastian proposes
to sell him for one. Thus the sea and its denizens repeatedly
slide into the texture of the play, as in the metaphor of fishing
for a comparison, the sea-shanty sung by Stephano, the sea-
marge where Ceres airs herself, Ariel's misdirecting mention
of the "still-vex'd Bermoothes," the threat to make a stockfish
of Trinculo. These are only a few of *Tmp.*'s ocean allusions;
many of them are subliminal, but they make the play more
redolent of sea-salt than any other of Shakespeare's. Not that
the sea invariably provides a poetic or a profound image.
Storms at sea may signify the tribulations of life, but stockfish
is stockfish, and it's not only a nice modern nostril that Poor
John would cause to wrinkle. Actually, the sea in *Tmp.* represents less the tribulations of life than an isolating, enclosing
element, most forcefully present in the first act and the last,
and making of the island a grassy stage for the working out
of conflicts that the characters bring from *outre-mer*. As often
in Shakespeare, exterior weather reflects the characters' psychological states; arriving in a whirlwind, the travellers depart with the assurance of calm seas and favoring winds. But
this is simply a natural sign of unclouded prospects. Apart

---

* Interestingly, he is neither black, brown, nor red of skin-tone. Perhaps,
being half-fish, he does not have a proper skin.

from the opening scene, in which the ocean acts mostly as an agent of the wizard, I cannot feel that the sea, for all its pervasive presence in the play, provides much more than atmosphere.

Even more potent in establishing a mood for *Tmp.* is the recurrent presence of music—more of it than in the other romances, which in turn contain more on average than Shakespeare's earlier plays. (The opera which it eventually became was a natural outcome of qualities in the play from the beginning.) No doubt the influence of the court masque should be noted here. As a relatively static pageant, the masque relied heavily on tableau, dance, and music; and a good deal of the music in *Tmp.* clusters around the tableau-scenes of the illusory banquet and the masque of the three goddesses. This is specifically mood music, "solemn and strange" for the banquet, and soft as prelude and probably background to the masque. Ariel, a spirit of the air, is given particularly airy songs to sing at the beginning and toward the end of the play; their elusive, mocking quality helps to create that sense of capricious, perhaps heartless, delight that distinguishes Ariel from the more solemn actors of the play—until, in V.17, he betrays for the first time humane solicitude. Ariel also uses song to lead, mislead, and occasionally to mock (after the fashion of Papageno in *The Magic Flute*) characters less volatile than he. The contrast with Caliban's barbaric chants of triumph at the end of Act II and briefly in III.ii is particularly enforced. "A howling monster, a drunken monster," says Trinculo in disgust; and it is true that Caliban does not compose very fine verses, but the impressive thing is that he composes verses at all.

'Ban, 'Ban, Cacaliban,
Has a new master, get a new man.
                              (II.ii.184 f.)

And in fact, like a truly Shakespearean monster, Caliban's exultant clangor manages to encompass a range of meanings and appended ironies. The "freedom" he celebrates is freedom to have a new master; and "get a new man" may either point at Prospero ("get a new servant") or imply that under a new master, Caliban will get (to be) a new man. It isn't a song to be racked for profundities, and it may be that the more confusion one finds in it, the better it will express Caliban's state of mind. Still, for the first composition of a monster in a high state of excitement, it's very creditable, and it prepares an audience to realize that everyone and everything on the island is in some degree musical, i.e., magic.

Though Shakespeare nowhere invites us to do so, it may be worth deliberately imposing on the play a fleeting connection between Caliban's speech on the musical island (III.ii.131) and Gonzalo's speech summarizing the moral plan behind the play's events (V.205). These two are the play's simpletons—not necessarily in being less intelligent than Stephano and Trinculo, for example, but in being mocked throughout for their naïveté. But Gonzalo, in trying to moralize the play's entire action, winds up as usual with his foot in his mouth, while Caliban, in articulating the sensual things that he alone knows, taps a special vein of poetry. His speech beginning

> Be not afeard; the isle is full of noises,
> Sounds and sweet airs, that give delight and hurt not.
>
> (III.ii.131 f.)

is especially impressive because nobody else in the play gives any evidence of hearing such music as he describes. No more, of course, does the audience. They are at one with the "natural" characters on stage in being excluded by their basic insensitivity from melodies that Caliban—not "mere" Caliban, but Caliban by virtue of his precious, unique faculties—hears all the time. For him the island twangles and hums continually with living music; after his speech a properly imaginative audience will be anticipating it, wondering about it, hoping it will be heard. The music we cannot hear—but might—will play on our imaginations or in them, it will render the island a tingling and continually animate experience.

On the other hand, Gonzalo's speech moralizing the action of the play (V.200 ff.) balances nicely between the old gentleman's moral decency and his mental obtuseness. He asks the gods to drop a blessed crown on the happy couple, unaware that in the masque they have already done so; he numbers among the triumphs of the voyage that Claribel found a husband at Tunis (we have been told she is wretched with him), that Prospero recovered his dukedom (though he had to take it away from brother Antonio); and (being still ignorant of the Antonio-Sebastian murder plot) that during their sojourn on the island,

> all of us (found) ourselves
> When no man was his own.

In worldly wisdom he is no less an innocent than he was in II.i, when Antonio and Sebastian made such merciless fun of him; good old simpleton that he is, he does not know, and never in the play does know, how close he and Alonso have come to having their weasands slit, or by whom. But his invincible simplicity has not prevented commentators from finding in this, his last major speech, something like the supreme message of the play. Providence, by turning all the apparent misfortunes of the early acts to a happy conclusion, has vindicated the essential beneficence of the universe, and brought each individual to a recognition of his true self. Seeming trials have proved to be blessings in disguise. *O felix culpa!*

But this seems to me piling hyperbole on extravagance. *All* comedies and many other modes of fictional action conclude happily after difficulties overcome; does this routine pattern make them all analogies to the fall and redemption of man? One comes close to obsession in thinking so. Besides, in the play before us, providence, far from showering its gifts freely and equally, has rather severely distinguished sheep from goats. Miranda may have found a new "self" and a new sphere of activity as Ferdinand's bride; just possibly Prospero has learned something new about being an effective duke. But everyone else goes back to his old self and his old round of activities, somewhat disadvantaged. Stephano never will be king of the island; he is going to be a butler for the rest of his days, and one to whom the keys of the wine-cellar will hardly be entrusted. Sebastian never will be king of Naples, can hardly even look for a position of minor trust around court. Antonio comes off worst of all, and indeed he should. The self he has found is that of a branded villain, as his sullen silence proclaims; his chances of legitimately inheriting the dukedom of Milan (even though legally he's still next in line from Prospero) are less than minimal. Whatever self he has found, he clearly doesn't like it. In short, "finding ourselves" may be—as in other contexts I have long suspected it would be—a very questionable experience, depending on the sort of self we find. And those are some of the dramatic reservations that lie behind Gonzalo's glad cry of "O rejoice beyond a common joy!" At the least, if he has gained new insight from his experiences on the island, it seems remarkably close to his old foolishness.

Allegorizing *Tmp.*, a favorite indoor sport dating from the 19th century, has largely run its course by the end of the 20th, and needs no further repudiation. Caliban as the Working Class (or alternatively the Missing Link), Ariel as the Poetic Imagination, Miranda as the Beatific Vision, and Prospero as Superman have had their day. The gentler formula that the island experience describes a rite of passage to a symbolic vision of an exalted and purified nature still flourishes. Though it applies rather awkwardly to prince Ferdinand and hardly at all to Stephano and Trinculo, its best chances of success lie in application to Alonso king of Naples. But it's to be noted that whatever vision he experiences must occur while he is off-stage, sunk in torpor or frenzy, within Prospero's magic circle in the line-grove. When he is released from this enchantment, he cannot describe what has been revealed to him within it, and does not even try to. Bottom the Weaver is more forthcoming than Alonso in describing his dream, though all he can say is that words are totally inadequate. And in fact it is a very strange sort of enlightenment which leaves Alonso, supposedly the story's central figure, ignorant to the end of his own brother's plot against his life.

That story titled "The Redemption of Alonso King of Naples," which some commentators evidently prefer to the story that Shakespeare presented under the title of "The Tempest," is but one of several grids that can be laid over the text by way of transforming it first and explaining it after. The play is a romance of recovery (like all three of the other romances) only if Prospero is at the center of it and only if the dukedom of Milan is thought to be worth recovering. To make Alonso's redemption from error the center of the drama goes against the apportionment of lines (under a hundred for Alonso, well over 500 for Prospero); goes against the idea of recovery, for Alonso, Sebastian, and Antonio are all losers by the return of Prospero; and goes against the dramatic emphasis which makes Alonso's conversion take place off-stage, silently, and without visible consequences except his offhand promissory note to behave better in the future.

Holding if we can to the text, it seems clear that what strikes Alonso to the soul is not a "learning experience," but the accusations of Prospero, spoken by Ariel in the denun-

ciation-scene, and amplified, as it seems to him, by the billows, the winds, and the thunder (III.iii.95). He is not
enlightened, he is terrified into confession; an apparently
supernatural agency has accused him. Maybe, like the Ancient Mariner, he will leave the island a sadder and a wiser
man, though happily Shakespeare does not say so, and in
leaving Antonio tight-lipped he seems deliberately to be
shading all the Sunday-school lessons latent in the play. As
for the "vision of a society permeated by the virtues of tol-
erance and forgiveness,"* I find no more reason to attribute
it to Alonso or Prospero than to Trinculo or the Boatswain.

Another reading of the play keeps the focus on Prospero,
but makes the crucial choice his internal one between "virtue
and vengeance" (V.28); and this is sometimes extended by
making the "virtue" in question specifically Christian. But
this pattern too fits only loosely over the play. Pagans beyond
number and believers other than Christian valued magnanimity as a virtue; and Prospero at the end of the play does
nothing and says little that can be remarked as "virtuous"
rather than "vengeful." The proles go back to their drudgery;
Caliban is left marooned on his island. Antonio, dispossessed
and publicly humiliated, faces a lifetime under the thumb of
suspicious Prospero; Sebastian can never again be sure how
much his brother knows or suspects. Without converting the
end of the play to a charnel-house, it's hard to imagine what
more Prospero could do by way of vengeance.

Given the standards of 20th century liberal democracy, the
new Duke of Milan is not in fact a very gentle or tolerant
figure. With the cruel history of chattel slavery behind us,
it's easy to exaggerate Prospero into an early instance of
"plantation mentality," his contempt for Caliban into the
brutal arrogance of the slave driver. But there's more than a
grain of rough truth in this perception, for those whose teeth

* Northrop Frye, Introduction to The Tempest (Pelican edition).

are set on edge by talk of universal toleration and forgiveness. The interpretive point is hardly a central one, but given the storm of moral idealism, blustering around *Tmp.*, anything that cuts down on humbug is for the good.

It is IV.i.188 before Prospero makes, almost in an aside, the play on words from which much interpretive speculation has sprung. Speaking of Caliban, he calls him

A devil, a born devil, on whose nature
Nurture can never stick; on whom my pains,
Humanely taken, all, all lost, quite lost.

The nature/nurture dilemma (which in modern phraseology is the heredity/environment debate) is posed for Caliban as early as the *dramatis personae*, where he is introduced as a "salvage and deformed slave." Of course when he was really "salvage," he was not a slave at all, as he says vigorously. So at least part of his cankered mind is what Prospero himself has made it; and, given a play where bilateral antitheses lie to hand as thick as pig-nuts, this one may be worth a moment's pursuit. Though it's no more than a metaphor, seeing Prospero and Caliban as super-ego and id or as father and son may suggest varieties of intimate interaction between two irreconcilable elements of an unbreakable unity—interaction that controls much of the play. Prospero and Caliban have been in the past equal explorers of the island, of Mother Nature, so to speak; Caliban then was teacher, Prospero pupil. "Then I lov'd thee," says Caliban, movingly, and with Miranda they might have made a sort of family, had it not been for the monster's lecherous attempt. Sex was the sin that destroyed that potential idyll, and since then Prospero has been the crabby, suspicious master, Caliban the sour, resentful servant. Yet something of the old relation lingers on, and at the end of the play (V.245) Prospero must admit

(like Gloucester saying ruefully, "the whoreson must be acknowledged,")

> this thing of darkness I
> Acknowledge mine.

Except in his native inclination to fall down and worship strangers, Caliban is not really a slave; he talks (I.ii.345) of being styed in a hard rock, but for all we can see is perfectly free to roam the island. The son of one sorcerer and stepson of another (though he trails about him only scraps and rags of supernatural awareness), he has once been king, and now bitterly resents his toil as the black guard of Prospero's cell. Yet he is not merely useful, he is necessary. "We cannot miss him," Prospero admits (I.ii.311); if he had not given occasion to be degraded, it might have been requisite to degrade him anyhow. Master and servant are among the most vitriolic and vociferous of Shakespeare's haters, yet they are also indispensable allies; without Caliban, Prospero would starve, without Prospero, Caliban might wind up in a Bartholomew Fair sideshow or on a fishmonger's barrow. It is inviting to think of them as very different offshoots of the same tangled root-system.

If this line of speculation, making of Prospero and his servant something more than flat antitheses, seems to soften if not obliterate some of the sharp contrasts between good magician and diabolic witch, I can't but think the better of it. "Ambiguous" is one term used above to describe Shakespeare's attitude toward Prospero's extraordinary powers; another could be "eclectic." Life on the island throbs to a deeper, more persistent rhythm than the back and forth of good and bad. Somewhere far to the rear of the Prospero-Caliban story lies a buried parallel with the myth of the Golden Age or the Garden of Eden—or for that matter the natural society half-described, half-imagined by Montaigne.

That paradise lost of natural sympathies was soundly ridiculed in II.i; but it lingers on, not only in the womb-like
languor of the island, but as background to the several reen-
actments of the Cain-Abel story contemplated in the play's
present actions. Perhaps in the pariah-figure of Caliban the
"civilized" characters can be thought to encounter, face to
face, a sacred and shameful ultimate of their own buried
selves. Thus the sense of illumination, beyond anything resulting from political adjustments in Milan, Naples, or wherever, with which the play concludes.

Under the heading of non-problems, one can dismiss geographical literalisms like the effort to define by latitude and
longitude the location of the island. Equally pedestrian is the
attempt to decide how Prospero and his infant daughter,
once smuggled out of Milan, were launched into a boat on
the high seas, which are some 75 miles distant. The byplay
over "widow Dido" in II.i need not be supposed to indicate
a systematic parallel with the *Aeneid*; it is quite well accounted
for as a passage at verbal arms, setting Gonzalo at odds with
the sarcastic wits who bait him. Prospero's epilogue, com-
paring the magician without his magic to the actor without
a role, concludes in conventional fashion by throwing the
speaker, and his enterprise the play, on the mercy of the
audience—mercy to be expressed by applause. That the final
lines refer to Shakespeare's prospective return to Stratford
or his anticipated reception into Abraham's bosom are wholly
unwarranted but otherwise harmless assumptions. If one
must have a farewell gesture at the end of Shakespeare's
career, better perhaps the simple act of deference traditional
to epilogues, which in its mock-submission to the audience
comes closest to a benediction.

Not even those who propose a bored and careless Shakespeare as author of the romances in general have had much
to say against the poetry of *Tmp.* Parts of the story-telling
he skimped. Prospero's briefing of Miranda on the family

background is a little hard to take, and the young people fall passionately in love at first sight in a way that suggest authorial impatience with the commonplace preliminaries. But the texture of *Tmp.*'s verse in its wonderful variety—from the hoarse impatience of the Boatswain in the storm, to the bell-like lyrics of Ariel, to the vital animism of Caliban, to the mild dignity of the masque, and the quiet, unemphatic speeches of reconciliation in Act V—bespeaks an artist fully possessed of his powers. Proclaiming to the world in all the formality of print that Shakespeare is an excellent writer feels like an empty exercise; but at least once, after experiencing such poetical riches, the most dour and businesslike of critics ought to testify to a sense of gratitude. Perhaps in these last plays Shakespeare relied more on his powers of evocation than on his skill as an architect; that puts particular pressure on his interpreters (meaning thereby all those who bestow on him the first gift of attention) not to respond in ways that are either bored or careless. He will renew us if we let him.

REFERENCES

A. D. Nuttall, *Two Concepts of Allegory* (New York, 1967), is primarily a hard-headed technical study in the logic of allegorical expression, but secondarily a sensitive appreciation of *Tmp.* It's to be expected that those who admire one part of Nuttall's book will be impatient of the other; but in this instance, following the argument precisely where one's instinctive sympathies do *not* lead will profit an adventurous reader.

A tantalizing commentary on *Tmp.* titled "The Sea and the Mirror" appears among the poems of W. H. Auden. I cannot pretend to understand all the preliminary lyrics and monologues; but the long prose discourse in which Caliban—having assumed for the moment some of the verbal mannerisms of the late Henry James—undertakes to act as the mirror or echo of the audience in reflecting on the reality/imagination dichotomy provides much material for inward meditation.

Richard Bernheimer's *Wild Men in the Middle Ages* (Harvard, 1952) assembles a great deal of curious lore about the wild man or woodwose, who certainly dates back to the 13th century and may well have entered into the concept of Caliban. Robert H. Goldsmith adds more material in "The Wild Man on the English Stage," *Modern Language Review* LIII, 4 (October, 1958).

Harry Berger, Jr.'s "Miraculous Harp" in *Shakespeare Studies* 5 (1969), p. 253, psychologizes Prospero sometimes brilliantly, sometimes to the near edge of the preposterous. More important than his animus against the mage (in which he follows a large tradition of Prospero-bashers) is his determined reluctance to see in the character's history any signs of learning from experience, any acquisition of practical and humanizing wisdom. This leaves the end of the play as written utterly incomprehensible, as one reduces *Measure for Measure* to a paltry, unpleasant action by denigrating too much the character of the Duke.

Robert West, in Chapter 6 of *Shakespeare and the Outer Mystery* (1968), discusses the ceremonial magic of Prospero, prudently emphasizing how very indefinite it is both in its operation and in its origins. By contrast, W. W. Curry in *Shakespeare's Philosophical Patterns* (1937/1959) predicates a wide and difficult range of Shakespearean reading—in Plotinus, Proclus, Porphyry, and Iamblichus—to account for qualities in Prospero that can be better explained without seeking so far.

VI

OPAQUE AND
TRANSPARENT

LIKE THE BIBLE, SHAKESPEARE'S TEXT TURNS AN OBLIGING
face to almost anyone who approaches it with a predetermined notion of what he wants to find there. The plays tell
stories of individual destinies in which major psychological
components are involved; they express overtly or implicitly
political, religious, and social attitudes; they invite and qualify sympathy judgments; they suggest historical and mythological analogies; strands of implied comparison and contrast
connect one play with the other. What the characters say on
stage can be taken in a variety of different ways; behind the
speeches may lie many different levels and tonalities of sym-
bolism or irony. Thus modern hermeneutics, with its ruling
passion for subsurface exploration, often faces Schliemann's
dilemma. Of the nine ruined cities piled one atop the other
at Troy, which is the city of Homer? Given the many levels
and patterns of meaning in Shakespeare, which are to be
seen through as transparencies, which are to be accepted as
opaque and conclusive? It isn't that the one "real" Troy is
any more present than the eight others; only that in terms

of certain preconceived interests (i.e., Homer's poem), it is live material, and the eight other Troys are inert.

So, in reading Shakespeare, just about everything that learned ingenuity can extract from the text is really there, at least *in potentia*. The tests come later. Can all discoveries serve equally the general ends of understanding and appreciation? Which effects do they enable, which preclude? How to minimize extraneous clutter while maximizing contact with the energies and harmonies for which the playwright was actually responsible? A critical mind must strike its own balance between overloading the text and underresponding to it; and in the ongoing, doubtless interminable, critical symposium, the pendulum of fashionable opinion will surely swing back and forth many times. But, whichever way it goes, we may profit from now and then trying to define as largely as possible what can be got from the texts themselves. If one were proposing that the texts can really be seen "by themselves," as an unchanging univocal statement, that would of course be overweening. But utter scepticism, no less than confident opinion, needs a measure of checking. That is what the critical symposium is supposed to provide; and "the text itself," though never an absolute fact, though not always a safe guide, may yet be an approximate rule. There is no other.

The romances, perhaps because they were considered for so long "secondary" Shakespeare, escaped for long the full brunt of interpretive pressure; but the last half century has more than made up. Perhaps as a result, the romances have now risen a bit in status; but the judgment rings a bit hollow, simply because there are not many comparable English plays against which to estimate them. Most students, and this one following them, see a marked difference between the first two and last two romances; but if *Per.* and *Cym.* both fall short of the ideal more fully achieved by *WT* and *Tmp.*, they do so for different reasons and in different measures. For all its *cheval-de-frise* of textual and structural problems, *Per.* gives intimations of vital and reviving forces behind its apparently flat tapestry action. Those forces are hidden behind too many veils for anyone to be sure whether their true locus is in Cerimon's natural magic, in Diana's patronage, in the wild, profound powers of the sea, or in the restored family circle; but that forces of renewal are felt, like magnetic fields, around the play and its predetermined action, is a potent fact. Either the topic kindled in his mind as Shakespeare wrote, or when he took over the play from other hands its potential opened before him. Had it been simply the "moldy tale" that Jonson called it, the last two of the four romances might never have been written. Though rough and unpromising, it is clearly the acorn from which the other romances grew.

Cym. is the most problematic of the four plays, and some define its problems as the uneasy mixture of politics and romance or the equally uneasy combination of primitive England as seen by Holinshed and renaissance Italy as seen by Boccaccio; but the effect in either case is that the play does not recede very far from its forestage stories. They are substantial stories, too: the Iachimo-betrayal, which could so easily turn to an Othello tragedy, the invasion of England by a greedy empire, the two royal sons lost in the wilderness for twenty years. Stories of such weight crush those vibrations of character that one would think most instinct with dramatic power. Not even the crucial turn of Posthumus' repentance is lightened by any real awareness of Imogen's meaning to him; and Pisanio is kept so busy with irrelevancies that Posthumus is spared the embarrassment of recognizing how much he owes to the better sense of his servant— though Imogen knows. Under the circumstances, Posthumus can hardly play more than the superficies of a man; even if in his escape from jealousy he came closer than he does to the ecclesiastical formula for penance, a formula is what it would still be. (Realistically speaking just for a moment,

Posthumus' first act on setting up a household with Imogen must be to dismiss Pisanio. He knows too much, Imogen knows too much, there is too much that will be impossible to forget; in him is foreshadowed the relation of Jeeves to Bertie Wooster. He will have to go, perhaps as servant to the newly bleached Iachimo.)

About WT and Tmp. enough has already been written by the assemblage of modern critics to show how extensively their suggestive powers have been recognized. Follies and extravagances imposed on these texts bear witness, no less than restrained and responsible criticism, to their aura. No question, they have inherited some favors from the bardolatry of the last two centuries. Some periods of English literature were quite deaf to their music. WT disappeared from the stage for a full hundred years till 1740, and the sort of clutter that was imposed both on it and Tmp. by revivalists shows clearly how little respect the two plays commanded.*
Yet both the quiet neglect and the more insidious "improvements" derived from the same stubborn literal-mindedness that Shakespeare in the romances themselves openly disdained. Flat statements of abstract antithetical contrast, such as Shakespeare went out of his way to avoid, the revisers of the 18th century trumpeted aloud; the nuances of imaginative fantasy they ironed flat. Even if Will Davenant didn't realize what he was doing in reducing Miranda to a sexual freak, Dryden might have had an inkling. That he didn't even recognize a problem evidences a major shift in the spiritual

* Though he professed great respect for Shakespeare, Dryden conspired with Davenant to balance Miranda—a woman who had never seen a man—with a male sexual curiosity—a man who had never seen a woman—in their "version" of Tmp. The busy farceurs also converted Sycorax from Caliban's mother to his sister, then added a couple of extra sailors and gave them an extra miscellaneous girl to leer at. After its resurrection, WT was often reduced on stage to the sheep-shearing scene with a few appended snippets from other parts of the play, or from other plays.

weather (the national sensibility, to give it a modern cant name) in the fifty-odd years since 1611.

When did that change get under way? Long before the Restoration, for sure; probably even before the polarizing of opinions that would lead imperceptibly into the civil war. Indeed, it seems arguable that Shakespeare's romances were out of style (or, which is the same thing, set a style of their own) even as they were being written. The taste of the times was changing (as it always is); but it is hard to find in the vicinity any plays by other authors that seem cast in the same mold as WT or Tmp. The old connection between Cym. and Philaster, which must have seemed to A. H. Thorndike when he proposed it in 1901 the easiest of all to make, has been knocked into a cocked hat by Harold S. Wilson.* Chronology is against it; even on the most schematic narrative terms, the two plays don't match at all well, and the more closely one looks at details—for example, the comparison of Imogen/Fidele with Euphrasia/Bellario—the more superificial the similarities seem, the deeper the differences. The reasons for the cross-dressing are different, the outcome is wholly different, the feelings generated are entirely different, the functions of the two episodes in the economy of their respective plays are diametrically different. The revelation of Bellario's true identity puts an end to Philaster's jealousy and silences Megra's malicious insinuations; the unmasking of Fidele amounts simply to the rediscovery of Imogen, a neater but also a less consequential episode as far as the untangling of the plot goes.

In terms of general structure, it is true that Philaster is closer to Cym. than to any of the other romances; but this is simply a way of saying that it is very unlike the other romances. Philaster is a drama of court intrigue in which, while an unjust

---

* Thorndike, *The Influence of Beaumont and Fletcher on Shakespeare* (1901); Wilson, *English Institute Essays* (1951).

usurper is dispossessed, the amours of four lovers (Philaster/ Arethusa, Pharamond/Megra), after many entanglements and cross-purposes, are sorted out. This court-intrigue plot is a regular favorite with Beaumont–Fletcher. Variations of it will be found in *The Maid's Tragedy* (Amintor/Aspatia, Evadne/ The King), in *A King and No King* (Arbaces/Panthea, Tigranes/ Spaconia), in *Valentinian* (Valentinian/Lucina, Maximus/Eudoxia), and in others too many to list. The Beaumont–Fletcher characters in these plays are participants in an intrigue, little else. Perhaps for one stunning moment Aspatia wraps herself in the mantle of forlorn Ariadne deserted by Theseus, but then she disappears till it is time for her to be killed in the middle of Act V. The other characters, and Aspatia herself after her moment, are defined by their parts in the immediate action—they suggest no larger significance, irradiate no self-imprisoned souls like Pericles or Leontes, play no games with the passage of time, carry about them no aura of the holy.

If the influence on Shakespeare of Beaumont–Fletcher— after absorbing for decades the attention of scholars—has at last foundered on the rocks of chronology and close analysis, very little attention has been given to influence flowing the other way. Perhaps it has seemed too obvious to need discussion. But some aspects of the influence can be usefully distinguished. The plays of Beaumont–Fletcher do draw now and then on Shakespeare's dramas, primarily for plot ideas. (Verbally, there is one distinct parallel between Perdita's speech in *WT* IV.iv.130–132 and Bellario's speech in *Philaster* IV.iv.4–6; though it's not definite who wrote first, a slight edge in priority probably goes to Beaumont–Fletcher.) Among the *Four Plays or Moral Representations in One* (probably 1608), "The Triumph of Love" bears some narrative resemblance to a part of *Measure for Measure* in that it concerns Gerrard and Violanta, unmarried lovers and subject to the death penalty whenever her pregnancy is discovered. The premise of *Cupid's Revenge* (probably 1612) is not unlike that

of *A Midsummer Night's Dream*, though it may also have roots
in the second book of Sidney's *Arcadia*; an angry god of love
causes princess Hidaspes to fall fatally in love with a grotesque dwarf, and produces other tragic mixups in the royal
court. Setting aside *The Woman's Prize* (1606?), which openly
derives from *The Taming of the Shrew*, *Rule a Wife and Have a
Wife* (1624?) reworks under minimal disguises and with some
extra materials the story of Kate and Petruchio. But these
parallels all concern the earlier plays of Shakespeare; there
is little or nothing from the romances. (And so one would
expect: working for the same company, linked in friendship,
the poets would not normally be peering over one another's
shoulders, each copying the other's current production.)
Once, however, Fletcher (working alone after Beaumont's
death in 1616) did lay hands on a Shakespearean romance,
and his handling of it indicates a very odd view of the
original.

The Sea Voyage (probably 1622)* can hardly be other than
an offshoot of *Tmp.* It begins with a storm at sea, and with
the casting ashore on a desert isle of the ship's company and
passengers. But at this point the author began to distance
himself from Shakespeare's play. The storm is a natural
storm, and the society on the island includes nobody resem-
bling Prospero, Miranda, Caliban, or Ariel. Rather, the gross
appetitive elements which Shakespeare almost completely
ignored are strongly emphasized. The desert island turns out
to contain mounds of gold and jewelry, over which the newly
shipwrecked company fall to fighting. More depressingly, it

---

* As the Beaumont–Fletcher plays were collected and published in folio
only in 1647, and the few earlier quarto printings stand in undefined
relation to the date of production (let alone composition), all chronology
is highly conjectural. Such guidance as I could get from the new edition
supervised by Fredson Bowers, I took. But since *Tmp.* had previously
been acted—so far as we know—only at court, its resurrection in print
for the First Folio may have made a parody of it particularly timely.

contains no foodstuff whatever, a lack that soon reduces the desperate castaways to thoughts of cannibalism. From this macabre alternative they are rescued (as people in Beaumont–Fletcher plays are always being rescued, in the nick of time) by discovering another society in another part of the island. This is a community of women who have forsworn all traffic with the other sex, but are getting impatient with a life of passionate celibacy. They fall with glad cries on the predominantly male party; and much heavy humor develops out of the ladies' inordinate desire for sex and the men's strong preference for food. A last-minute reprieve from mass-execution, a scattering of happy recognition scenes, and the promise of domestic bliss for everyone bring the play to a close.

Probably the contriver of The Sea Voyage intended it as a direct burlesque of Tmp.; that in itself suggests that Shakespeare's play was felt to be excessively removed from the "real" world and its scrimmage of appetites. Whether deliberately sardonic or not, The Sea Voyage didn't strike Dryden, who saw clearly its dependence on Tmp., as implying ridicule. This says a lot about the mind-set with which Dryden and his contemporaries read Tmp. Likely as not, he saw the two plays as adventure stories on about the same level—especially after he and Davenant had finished their work of improving Tmp. The nuances of Shakespeare's original text—not just those propounded by modern criticism but those that were apparent to the early 19th century—had to be sandpapered down for restoration tastes to create a much blunter and broader play. And Dryden, if he noticed the difference at all, didn't think it worthy of remark.

The plays of Fletcher, Beaumont-and-Fletcher, and Fletcher-with-somebody-else are a world in themselves, and a various one; but it can't be sampled across the board, taking plays of different authors and different genres from different periods, without a strong sense of honest opaque carpentry that's alien alike to the concentrated fury of the high Shake-spearean tragedies and the wide-encroaching wonder of the romances. Indeed, the early plays, including Beaumont's superb burlesque, *The Knight of the Burning Pestle* (1607–08), and that fragile, poetic failure *The Faithful Shepherdess* (1610), have the romances and their dream-like atmosphere very much in mind. The chivalric romance is ridiculed for its incoherent structure, and the pastoral romance accommodates itself easily to a minimal silly plot. But when they hit their stride, Beaumont–Fletcher produced as a rule thoroughly well-made plays which are never subjected to excess pressure from their thoroughly domesticated themes. For example, *The Island Princess* (1621), despite its exotic setting (a Portuguese colony in India), is thoroughly mechanical in its intrigue. The chivalric Portuguese adventurer outdoes the prudent one for the princess' hand; they combine to repel the treacherous wiles of the blackhearted enemy Governor disguised as a pagan priest who would rob them of their Christian faith. Extended struggle against a remorseless villain climaxed by a series of triumphant fifth-act reversals is a frequent feature of these later plays. It is a formula in which the characters, each marked by a single humor or mannerism, define themselves within the framework of a particularly opaque plot—one that seems to devour much of their individuality and damp any vibrations of which they may be capable. Various in many other respects, plays like *Cupid's Revenge* (1615), *Valentinian* (1610–14?), and *The Loyal Subject* (1618?) all partake of this character. Even comedies like *The Wild Goose Chase* (1621) or *The Humorous Lieutenant* (1619) devote themselves to purging the principal characters of their predominant humors, sometimes quite mechanically, as in the last-named play. The impression is far stronger of the square than of the mysterious, of an inspiration from Jonson's satirico-realistic comedies than from anything like Shakespearean romance.

From Act I, scene i, line 1 of *The Wild Goose Chase* it is clear that Mirabell is going to be caught by Oriana after four and a half acts of deception, elusion, and delay; when the time is ripe, his two marionette-companions will fall into line just as inevitably. What sort of marriage will develop out of this disguising and trapping? There is no more reason to ask the question than to care about the domestic routines of Punch and Judy. It is true that querulous critics have been concerned lest Miranda as princess of Naples get bored or disillusioned with the society of that city—or that Perdita will not be satisfied with bearing a succession of sturdy children to Florizel (who cannot fail to remind us of the Prince of Monaco). But these are marriages founded on what we must accept as straightforward mutual affection, not cynical entrapments and the kind of choosing up sides that amounts to pointing a finger and saying, "You go with you and she gets him; now is there anybody left over?" This is courtship comedy in which the only fixed principle is that the numbers come out even. During the Restoration, *The Wild Goose Chase* enjoyed great popularity; it became a model for the pairing-off, squaring-off sex comedy.

(One would like to know, on a basis more secure than impressions, whether the sort of underlining, trimming, and squaring off that was practiced through the 18th century on the plays of Shakespeare was felt to be equally necessary in adapting the plays of Jonson, Beaumont–Fletcher, and their several collaborators. Such a comparative study, extending the pointed analyses of Norman Rabkin in *Shakespeare and the Problem of Meaning* [Chicago, 1981], would provide a strong index to the expectations and standards of explicit statement that enlightened audiences brought to the theater and recognized as missing in earlier work.)

Calling anything the "first," "last," or "only" one of its kind invites instant refutation; and of course the mode of romance as one of the permanent, pervasive tonalities available to the human imagination always turns out simply to have shifted shape when we think it has faded away. After Shakespeare, romance in England modulates into new keys with Milton, Bunyan, the spiritual autobiographies, and the corrosive burlesque of Butler; before the century's end romance in France will have gathered its energies to produce one of the most influential of early novels, *La Princesse de Clèves*. Anyone can make his own list of the forms and styles to which the spirit of romance has successively attached itself down to the present day when smarmy semi-erotic fictions are listed on drugstore shelves as "romances" plain and simple. But on the English stage after the four Shakespeare romances there does not seem to be anything comparable for a long time to come. Perhaps the spaced-out episodic plot, which was evidently a staging problem from the beginning, proved to be such a difficulty as only the poetic gifts of Shakespeare could surmount. In any event, the Shakespeare romances remained, like many exotic plants, infertile. They stand apart in a garden, not by any means of leeks and cabbages, but of plants less rare and finely inbred than they are. Secluded in their creation from Shakespeare's other plays, they have remained a half-covert and somewhat special field of taste. There is nothing quite like them.

One of the qualities that for long kept the romances in the background of Shakespeare's achievement is that they don't put up a good front: in a variety of different ways they shake, or threaten to shake, an audience out of the accustomed cradle of make-believe. The curtain of pretence is flimsy and often (it would seem) deliberately tatty. But in a modernist or (for some) a post-modernist world, the old fault has become a new virtue. Since all the façades are down—on the stage, as just about everywhere else—it's now easy to appreciate translucence. To know what's enough and not too much is, evidently, less easy, and I have no snap formula. But the field lies open to adventurers.

As applied to literature, "translucence" is a relative, not an absolute, quality, and as a value term it is far from univocal; it may be applied to a blur or smear as well as a focussed effect. But it points to a quality repeatedly stressed in discussing the romances; a quality of seeing through characters without ceasing to see them, of moving in one direction with the logic of statement and in others with devices of allusion and implication. Translucence is felt along that network of unspoken forces that bind the strong points of a composition into a constellation. No doubt this quality of surpassingly doubled language was Shakespeare's from the beginning; the romances, for whatever reasons, invited it to flower. In experiencing these plays one wants, so far as possible, to know the fullness of the various harmonies, strained free of the prosthetics and adulterants of modern prepossession. The double process requires that some very pretty notions have their necks wrung. But the enterprise itself is rare and high. For the voices that Shakespeare wove together in this quartet of plays make up a strain of intimate, implicative utterance the like of which has never since been heard on the English stage.

APPENDIX:
THE POST-ROMANCE,
PERHAPS-
SHAKESPEAREAN
PLAYS

AFTER COMPLETING THE ROMANCES, SHAKESPEARE MAY HAVE taken a hand in the writing of three other plays, which call for an accounting here.

Cardenio

Cervantes' novel *Don Quixote* was published at Madrid, the first part in 1605, the second part ten years later; it spread rapidly across Spain and Europe, and a translation of Part I into English appeared in 1612. One of the interpolated stories occupying several chapters of that first part concerns the adventures of Cardenio and Lucinda, which are entangled with the simultaneous adventures of Fernando and Dorothea. This may have provided material for a play in which Shakespeare collaborated with John Fletcher. There can be no doubt, in view of his involvement with the strongly Quixotic *Knight of the Burning Pestle* (1607–1608) that Fletcher knew Cervantes' novel, and knew it well.

In May and July of 1613, a play titled *Cardenno* or *Cardenna* was presented at court by the King's Men; and in 1653 the publisher Humphrey Moseley registered (but did not publish) a number of old plays including *The History of Cardenio*, authorship of which he ascribed to Fletcher and Shakespeare. After that the play disappears from view till 1728, when Lewis Theobald published a play, *Double Falsehood or the Distrest Lovers*, which he said was "revised and adapted" from one originally written by Shakespeare. The play thus brought forward does bear a very broad narrative similarity to the story told by Cervantes, in that it rearranges the affairs of four lovers. How it relates to the hypothetical Fletcher–Shakespeare version cannot be told, for though Theobald said he had a script of that play, it was never offered to public inspection, let alone published; and in 1808 the manuscript, if it actually existed, was destroyed by fire. Perhaps if *Double Falsehood*, which actually did get published, showed any strikingly Shakespearean traits of language or of character, it might have some claim to a place on the outer fringe of the Shakespeare canon. But it does not even contain a character named "Cardenio"; if related at all to a semi-Shakespearean original, it is so remotely related as to have lost all savor of what it might have been.

The Two Noble Kinsmen

When or where *The Two Noble Kinsmen*, probably by Fletcher and Shakespeare, appeared on the stage cannot be known for sure—nor, accordingly, can anything more than a guess be hazarded as to when it was written. Not included in the First Folio, it first appeared in print in 1634. One piece of material interpolated in the basic story, the morris-dance of III.v, has been thought to derive from a work of Beaumont, *The Masque of the Inner Temple and Gray's Inn*, performed before James I on February 20, 1613. At least conjecturally, that sets a *terminus ante quem*.

As the prologue makes explicit, the source of the play was Chaucer. The knight's tale, i.e. the story of Palamon and Arcite, provides material for the main, and indeed almost the only, plot. Act I, in which the three queens petition Theseus at length to help them against the tyrant Creon, is greatly enlarged from Chaucer; for the subplot of the gaoler's daughter who liberates Palamon from prison and then runs mad for love of him there is no Chaucerian warrant at all; and the morris dance of the schoolmaster and villagers, noted above, is also interpolated material.

Even though the many years of Chaucer's narrative were compressed on stage to much, much less material, stuffing was needed because the heroes, Palamon and Arcite, are so remarkably inflexible in their attitudes—their inner resolution neither changes nor wavers from beginning to end. There are fine ironic scenes when their basic magnanimity and mutual devotion are sorely tested by their unflinching rivalry for the hand of Emilia. But as the play is one long impasse, it must be perceptibly stretched, if only for the sake of richness and variety; and two pieces of the inserted material suggest a possibly important theme.

After the three queens have successfully asked for Theseus' aid in defeating Creon and enabling them to bury their dead husbands, Hippolyta and Emilia are drawn, by a discussion of the friendship of Theseus and Pirithuous, to describe Emilia's girlhood friendship with one Flavinia. It was an intimate innocent friendship, but absorbing enough, even in memory, to have left Emilia with a strong distaste for matrimony, which she expresses to Hippolyta. The occasion is not exactly opportune, since Hippolyta is herself on the threshold of marriage; but the point is made, and it establishes a basic irony of the drama, that the lady over whom Palamon and Arcite—loving and admiring cousins—carry on such a violent and passionate feud is not only indifferent as between them, but finds men as such actively distasteful. In our degenerate and outspoken days, the thought would naturally arise as to whether her inclinations are Lesbian; but of that the play gives no indication. She is simply cold; her ideal of a relation is that childhood friendship with Flavinia—who, having been mentioned this once, disappears permanently from the play.

The other curious insert has to do with the story of the gaoler's daughter, who is smitten with a very grown-up passion for Palamon, and releases him from prison in order to flee with him into the woods where she hopes to get him to marry her, or something. Frustrated in these lascivious designs, she grows distracted, and after some wandering about returns to her father, who on the advice of a physician persuades her previous lover to personate Palamon and sleep with her. Nothing, he says confidently, will be better for her frazzled nerves. Apparently he is right. A soothing bout of sexual exercise works wonders for the young lady; we can guess for ourselves what she said in the morning, and in any case it doesn't matter, because she disappears from the play for good. Sexual desire, it appears, is a kind of madness, for which (by good fortune) any random member of the opposite sex possesses an easy cure. No wonder, we may think, if Emilia prefers her girlish friendship with Flavinia; and no wonder if the passion of Palamon and Arcite for Emilia destroys the finest thing their lives contain, that is, their devotion to each other.

From this angle, *The Two Noble Kinsmen* appears as an antiromantic romance; and that, though in the working out of the story Emilia had to be warmed up a bit, seems to have been its original design. Though it's hard to delimit the areas and define the degrees of control by Chaucer, Fletcher, and Shakespeare, if one puts the play in a Shakespeare context it reveals a number of interesting reverbations with earlier treatments of white innocence and the darker consequences of sexual passion. Shakespeare's choice of the Chaucerian story in the first place—if it was his choice—is harder to explain. Making an anti-romance out of an authentic, recognizable knighthood-and-ladyship romance may have appealed to the playwright as a *tour de force*; plainly the two-dimensional story offered him little scope for Shakespearean character development, and the idea of a love story with a frigid heroine perhaps provoked him, if only by its difficulties. One is perhaps less encumbered by the opposite hypothesis, that the original idea for the play was Fletcher's. In any event, whatever parts of *The Two Noble Kinsmen* are assignable to Shakespeare, the flip-flop ending, in which Emilia is dealt off first to one noble knight and then to his Tweedledee alternative, comes close to reducing the entire story to a self-parody. It may be Shakespeare, but it's not prime Shakespeare.

The Famous History of the Life of King Henry the Eighth

Just about everything connected with this play, from its title to its authorship, is subject to question; the few unchallengeable facts first. The date and place of one production we know because on June 29, 1613, during a performance of this play, the Globe theater was set on fire and burned to the ground. The text of the play was included in the 1623 First Folio as entirely the work of Shakespeare, and though persistent doubts have been expressed that it may be a work of collaboration with John Fletcher, proof positive has yet to be established either way. Several contemporary accounts—which do not, however, name Shakespeare or anyone else as the author—say the play was "new" when some of its special effects set fire to the playhouse; and they specify its title as *All Is True*. The alternate title may have been intended to distinguish an historical play, based upon the chronicles, from a fantastic drama about Henry VIII, assembled by one Samuel Rowley of the Admiral's Company, titled *When You See Me, You Know Me*, and presented in 1603. In the great Folio of 1623, *Henry VIII* was placed last among the histories, and is the only one of that group containing the word "history" in its title.

Though the question of authorship, after nearly a century and a half of discussion, seems no closer now than it ever was to final solution, the units of the play attributed to Shakespeare by James Spedding in 1850, and most often used as the basis for analysis, are:

I.i, ii: the downfall of Buckingham, and Catherine's plea against exactions
II.iii, iv: Anne Boleyn and the old lady; the "trial" of Catherine
III.ii, 1–203: the king's anger with Wolsey
V.i: Cranmer's private interview with the king

This division of the play is based on metrical and linguistic tests which are not always more reliable as they are more sensitive; the nature of the arrangement which assigned the most distinguished playwright of his age to write preparatory and introductory scenes, while a relative novice assumed the strong dramatic contrasts to which they lead, every individual must imagine for himself.

The play itself, while very much a processional of tableaux vivants and pageants (as everyone has remarked), comprises an artful and ultimately potent evocation of moralized history. It is akin to Jonson's *Sejanus* (1603) in that a Damocles' sword, the unpredictable, irresistible whim of a despot, hangs over the heads of the characters throughout. A series of unjust or clearly arbitrary decisions mark the first part; Buckingham's fall and the crafty maneuverings to deprive honorable queen Catherine of her marriage accumulate guilt on Cardinal Wolsey. His fall when it occurs is greeted on stage at first with vindictive exultation; but his own comportment under misfortune, underlined by the sympathetic responses of Cromwell, Griffith, and the long-suffering queen herself, does much to balance an audience's feelings. The story of Cranmer turning the tables on the council at the last minute by producing the king's ring illustrates in capsule and highly dramatic form the instability of court fortunes. Thereafter the play turns to celebrating the arrival of Elizabeth, who will bestow on the kingdom the crowning blessings of James: it is like a historical masque in which all the ultimates take tangible form to bless the audience.*

Over the years, *Henry VIII* has proved itself an imposing stage processional pointing up a pattern of injustice and wrong working themselves out to ultimate good. This can very easily be seen, if one gives the concluding rhetoric all it asks for, as the triumphant climax of the entire sequence of historical plays. Whether Shakespeare conceived of his "historical" plays as such an all-encompassing sequence (it

---

* Felperin argues (*Shakespearean Romance*, Chap. 6) that Buckingham, Katherine, and Wolsey, by redeeming their material catastrophes with a measure of spiritual edification, enact a series of fortunate falls, and so give to *Henry VIII* a more "romance" flavor than can be found in the other history plays. It is peculiar that a feature which never occurs in the unquestioned romances should be cited as evidence of romance influence on *Henry VIII*. In the other direction, the whole mystique of the elect nation, long held in bondage to antichrist but redeemed by its own glorious virtues, was a collectively composed national romance, almost a national romance *trouvé*. But the structure of Shakespeare's play does not enact the pattern of a quest or recovery, does not represent a solitary adventure, involves neither love nor battle nor hardship nor travel to exotic places; it has none of the traditional romantic ingredients. To inscribe *Henry VIII* among the romances is a work of strong prepossession eked out with desperate ingenuity.

was fourteen years since he wrote the last one), or indeed whether he ever thought of "history plays" as a sub-group, may be questioned. One sure thing is that *Henry VIII*, whoever wrote it and in whatever context we view it, has precious little to do with the romances. "All is true" alone marks it as of another world, a world apart from Pentapolis, Sicilia, and that rarer island where Caliban still snuffles in the mud, snaring the nimble marmoset, and dreaming of something wonderful in the clouds that strains our imaginations to conceive. Mopsa, Dorcas, and their ilk will make up the audience of a play to which the subtitle "all is true" most naturally appeals.